LIFE AND SUICIDE SOMETHING TO TALK ABOUT

ENRIQUE M. TORDILLO JR

LCCN Number : 2025932221

Contents

ON MY DYING DAY

Growing up, I leaned heavily toward pessimism. Life always seemed like a series of obstacles, and I carried a mindset that expected failure or disappointment at every turn. My negativity wasn't without cause—personal struggles, societal pressures, and an overall sense of unease shaped my view of the world.

Things came to a head when I entered adulthood, got married, and started a family. What should have been a joyful chapter of my life was riddled with financial struggles and marital problems that nearly cost me everything. There were moments when it felt like the weight of the world was crushing me, leaving me paralyzed with doubt, fear, and despair. I felt lost, isolated, and unable to see a way forward.

Then came a pivotal moment—a day when the burden became too great to bear. With my back against the wall, I made a decision that changed my life forever. I surrendered. Not to my problems, but to something greater. Although I had never been deeply religious, I turned to God in my darkest hour, offering up all my worries, fears, and frustrations. I prayed—not in desperation, but in a spirit of gratitude and trust.

It wasn't an immediate transformation, nor did my circumstances magically improve overnight. Financial troubles persisted, and life's challenges didn't suddenly vanish. But something within me shifted. Through daily prayers, often whispered in the solitude of my car during drives to work, I found a newfound sense of peace. I thanked God for the blessings I had—big and small—and reaffirmed my faith that brighter days were ahead.

This act of surrender was transformative. It was less about religion and more about cultivating gratitude and hope. My problems didn't go away, but my approach to them changed. Instead of dwelling on the negative, I learned to face challenges with resilience and a belief that everything happens for a reason.

THE DEVIL

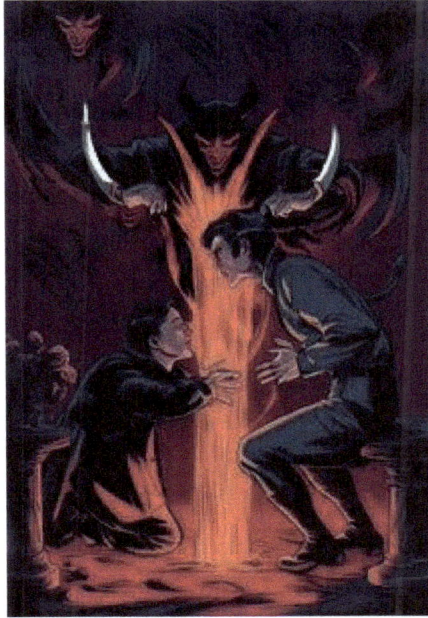

Who is the devil? In my opinion, the devil resides within us. It is a creation of our own minds, manifested into reality. The devil constantly whispers in our ears, tempting us to do terrible things. If we allow it to influence our actions, then it has us in its grasp. Bad things are a choice; we either do it or we don't. We hear it all the time, and we see it all the time that people do bad things, thinking they can get away with it; we know when we are doing something wrong, we feel it, and our mind tells us that it is terrible, our body sends a signal to its veins warning us. The devil is real, in my view. Just look at the war and hatred in the world.

Some people in power are driven by greed. I believe the world would be a much better place without this greed. Instead of helping others, those in power often choose to enrich themselves. Whenever we do illegal drugs and consume alcohol, it empowers the devil within us; alcohol and drugs send our brain into a tailspin, we lose ourselves and let the devil take over, and once we sober up and the damage has been done, you can't undo it.

When faced with the temptation of drugs or alcohol, we know the right choice is to say no. Overcoming substance abuse is far from easy, but it's important to remember what happened the last time you gave in— it didn't end well. Why go down that path again? For many, addiction is a sickness, and recognizing it in yourself is the first step. Seek help and reach out, because staying silent only lets the problem grow.

Don't let the devil win by pulling you into poor choices. Instead, invite God into your life. By doing so, you can find strength, clarity, and peace—mentally, physically, and emotionally. Surrender your struggles to God, and you'll discover a better path forward.

GRATIFICATION

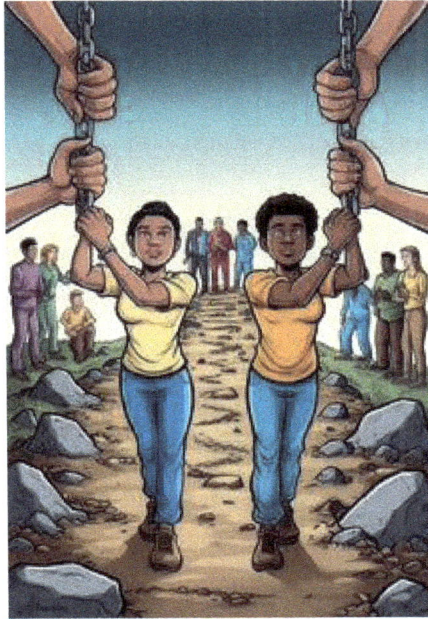

Choosing life over death brings a sense of happiness and fulfillment—something I know from personal experience. This choice doesn't eliminate challenges, but it changes how we face them. We come to understand that difficulties are part of the journey, but instead of stressing or getting angry, we learn from them. Like studying history in a textbook, we reflect on our own past, recognize where we went wrong, and grow from it.

It's okay to learn from your mistakes, they're part of your story. Gratification in life is not given. It's earned. There's nothing more fulfilling than achieving something for which we've worked so hard. No one can take that away from you. That diploma you earned in school to improve your life? It's yours for life. The titles before your name—whether officer, supervisor, manager, or doctor—are a testament to your effort, and you absolutely deserve them. Anything you work for the end is a gratification, and you will not see that if you take your life away. The challenges in life are not meant to give you a hard time; they are intended to teach you something. It is a meaningful education. Remember Thomas Edison? The great inventor? They didn't call him "the wizard" overnight. He failed a thousand times before inventing the light bulb, which he created over a century ago, yet we still benefit from that invention today. All the hard work you're putting in now—whether big or small—matters. There's no such thing as insignificant effort; it will eventually add up and become something truly significant.

Let's call it what it is: suicidal tendencies are a significant aspect of mental illness, and if left untreated, they can worsen. Sometimes we become so focused on our problems that we overlook their root cause: our minds. We might believe we're processing these issues correctly, but often we're mistaken. We think we've explored all avenues to escape our sinkhole, yet we remain trapped.

I'm writing this book because I want to share what I have experienced, suicidal thoughts, so I can relate if a person is having the feeling of hopelessness.

DISAPPOINTMENTS

Can you imagine a world without disappointment? Anything you want, you get a house, cars, girlfriend/boyfriend, wife/husband, jobs or even business. It would be a beautiful world if that were true, but the reality is that disappointment is inevitable and can happen to the best of us. In life, disappointment is something we must expect from time to time, and learning to accept it is crucial. It doesn't mean you won't get what you want—sometimes, it just takes longer than expected, or it arrives in a different form, often better than what you originally imagined.

For example, I wanted to be a police officer, and I got denied or didn't get the position, but only to have an opportunity to become a federal officer of the government instead, so my wish to become a police officer got upgraded to a better job opportunity. I believe in the phrase, "When one door closes, another one opens." In my experience, this has often been true. Sometimes, when you reflect, you realize we might be destined for something better than what we originally hoped for or planned. Sure, there were missed opportunities in my life that I wish I had seized, but I can't dwell on the past. Every morning I wake up is a new blessing—a fresh start, a new hope, and another chance to do something different or better.

Disappointment should not always be taken negatively in your life; we also should take it as a learning event of why we didn't get that job that we wanted; maybe we are not qualified enough, so let's prepare ourselves for the next opportunity. Another example is when you don't get the man or woman you wanted, only to realize later that they weren't right for you. In the end, you might find yourself with a much better partner. I truly believe that if something isn't meant for you, then it's simply not meant to be. God knows what's best for you, even when it's hard to see at the moment.

LIFELINE/MENTAL ILLNESS:

Why do we have to talk about it? It's funny we even have to ask. As if it is taboo, the good news is that talking about mental illness is now a common thing because mental illness is recognized as an actual ailment or a disease. Most health insurance nowadays offers it for you. The government and state programs also offer free mental health services. You can reach out to the national suicide and crisis lifeline by calling 988 or 1-800-273-8255. Research indicates that callers often feel less suicidal, less depressed, less overwhelmed, and more hopeful after speaking with a lifeline counselor. Whatever state or country you are in, there is help you can reach out to; also, one source of help you can go to is the internet.

You can access the services you need from the comfort of your own home. Engaging in conversation with someone can awaken your mind to a wealth of knowledge you never knew existed. Don't shut yourself off just because you lack the answers—stay open-minded. We all tackle our problems differently, but let's strive to prevent our issues from escalating further. That's how we should tackle our problems: not to make them worse.

SUICIDE

Why do we have to talk about it? Do you know the phrase "what if?" "Should have" and "could have" are not going to materialize, and you will never know because you have ended your life. As I mentioned, I can relate because I've been in that situation. But you know what? Now I can answer all those questions, like "What ifs" and "What could have been." Being alive allows me to reflect on those lost spirits or souls still wandering among the living. They remain trapped in their thoughts, unable to transition from the land of the living to the dead because, unfortunately, it's too late for them. And I wouldn't be sharing this experience with you if I had not made that fatal mistake. Growing up as a child, I felt alone, but that is not always the case, maybe because I want to prove something to myself.

Why is it important to discuss mental health issues? There's a saying: "What the mind says, the body will follow." With the increasing demands we place on ourselves—our needs, expectations, and responsibilities—many of us find ourselves carrying burdens that can feel overwhelming. I know I've fallen into that trap as well; I often push myself beyond my limits as an overachiever. It seems I can't help but strive for better. Life is indeed full of challenges. But, is that a bad thing? To challenge yourself to be better? If your intention is for the good and your heart truly believes it, go for it.

Quote: THROUGH THE STORM, YOU HAVE TO BELIEVE IN YOURSELF; NO MATTER WHAT THEY SAY, BELIEVE IN YOUR FAITH.

Look at the news; you see an actual zombie in the streets because of illegal drugs, out of their mind, out of sanity. Problems, whether big or small, can quickly escalate into situations we'd rather avoid. When faced with a challenge, it's crucial to confront it head-on.

Resorting to alcohol or illegal drugs won't provide a solution—we all know this deep down, yet we often choose to ignore it. But here's the reality: those problems will still be there waiting for us when we wake up the next morning.

ROAD RAGES

Road rage has become increasingly common, and it seems to worsen every year, leading to more accidents on our streets and roads. I believe this rise is closely tied to mental health, which impacts our judgment and reactions. It's a frightening reality and a stark reminder of how quickly things can go wrong on the road.

Staying aware of your surroundings and remaining alert is crucial in these situations. Defensive driving is equally important—while we can't control others' actions, we can control how we respond. Reacting calmly and prioritizing safety can make all the difference. Remember, safety should always come first!

At first, I was furious and chased the vehicle, determined to confront the driver. When I caught up, I stopped by his side, looked him in the eyes, and showed my anger. But he just looked back at me, confused, as if he didn't even know what had upset me. In that moment, I realized

I should have been grateful—nothing terrible had happened. Reacting with anger could have made the situation far worse, fueled by my own emotions.

I prayed and thanked God for keeping the situation from escalating. Accidents can happen at any moment, beyond our control—that's why they're called accidents. Letting anger take over would have only added to the chaos. Instead, I learned the importance of taking a deep breath and appreciating that nothing serious occurred. It could have been so much worse, and for that, I'm grateful.

Quote: I AM THANKFUL EVERY DAY FOR WHAT I HAVE BECAUSE I KNOW SOMEONE IS LESS FORTUNATE THAN ME.

Tragedy is often too much to bear; no one should ever experience it, yet it happened. Healing can take a long time and is often unbearable, but you know what? You don't have to navigate this journey of recovery alone; there's plenty of support available. Remember the saying, "The pain may fade, but the scar remains." Those scars serve as reminders of people or events in our lives. But that's all they are— reminders or memories of the past. Rising from a tragedy can be a powerful experience and a source of motivation. I choose to focus on the positive aspects of life, believing in the saying, "What doesn't kill you makes you stronger."

After enduring a tough experience, dwelling on negativity won't help you heal; instead, try to channel that energy into something uplifting.

Get Up! Rise! Say you're self "I can do it" sounds cliché, but it works.

THE VALUE OF LIFE

Sometimes, people feel isolated, believing no one truly cares about them. This misconception can lead to despair, yet we are never as alone as we think. Every human connection—whether it's a family member asking about our day or a stranger giving a simple nod of acknowledgment—shows that others do care, even in small ways. The man in the story felt unseen, but when he examined his life, he saw that people did care about him; he had just overlooked these gestures.

Many of us carry hidden burdens, doubting if anyone would notice our disappearance, but often, these are illusions our minds create. We must strive to recognize the signs of love and kindness around us.

In our last moments, as we reflect, we ask ourselves profound questions: Have we made the most of our time? Have we left behind something meaningful? If we wait, it may be too late to make changes. So, while we're alive, let's do our best with the life we have. Each day offers a chance to create meaning, to show kindness, and to leave the world better than we found it.

Life isn't about perfection but progress. Mistakes and struggles are a part of the journey, teaching us valuable lessons for those willing to learn. Don't wait until it's too late to embrace your life and those around you. Choose to make your today meaningful; however small the actions may seem.

Reflecting on life's true value often leads us to examine our legacy. Beyond wealth or accolades, legacy includes the relationships we nurture, the kindness we extend, and the knowledge we pass on. Consider how acts of generosity, no matter how small, become part of a lasting ripple effect, creating memories that outlive us and inspire others. By living with intention, each person has the power to contribute to a broader purpose, investing in the community and cultivating an atmosphere of support.

Our resilience in life—how we face difficulties and yet continue to strive—adds to this legacy. An act of kindness may renew their strength and belief in humanity. Life's true worth often reveals itself in these connected experiences, proving that we're all part of a larger story that thrives on compassion, courage, and hope.

STOP FEELING SORRY FOR YOURSELF

There's a point when we have to stop dwelling on our problems and take control. Self-pity traps us in a cycle of negativity, convincing us that we're powerless. But we're stronger than we think. Self-doubt and despair are persistent, whispering that we're not good enough or that things will never improve. These thoughts may feel real, but they're often exaggerated reflections of our fears.

Instead, take one small step forward. Action breaks the chains of self-pity. Every positive choice builds momentum, moving us toward a better future. When we stop focusing on our perceived limitations, we begin to see possibilities. Strength comes from facing challenges head-on. There will be setbacks, but they're only temporary. We must push through, learn from our experiences, and keep moving forward.

Self-pity, though natural, can be a trap. When we're stuck in a cycle of negative thoughts, we lose sight of the fact that we can overcome hardships. But breaking free from this mindset requires effort and honesty. It involves recognizing when we wallow in our struggles and shifting our focus to solutions, however small they may seem. Each step we take, however incremental, proves our capability to progress.

Life will always throw challenges our way, but it's our response that defines us. Learning to move past self-pity doesn't mean ignoring our emotions; instead choosing to act despite them. Resilience is about bouncing back from adversity, finding ways to adapt, and remaining open to change. Taking accountability for our lives refusing to be passive victims, is empowering. It shifts the focus from what's wrong to what's possible, creating a mindset seeking opportunities for growth, even through tough times.

THE DEVIL WITHIN:

We often hear about the "inner demons" that everyone faces, including jealousy, fear, or even resentment. However, one of the most productive ways to confront this "devil within" is through self-compassion and understanding. Self-compassion doesn't mean accepting poor behavior; rather, it allows us to investigate the reasons behind our thoughts and actions. Often, these darker aspects arise from insecurities or past events. By recognizing them, we can choose healthier ways to address these feelings.

Consider someone whose jealousy leads them to compare themselves negatively with others. By recognizing this emotion, they can transform it into a motivation for self-improvement rather than harboring resentment. This act of inner alchemy—turning a negative feeling into a means for personal growth—is how we can combat the "devil" effectively. When we learn to navigate our emotions without judgment, we cultivate inner peace, strengthening our control over harmful impulses and fostering a deeper understanding of ourselves.

The concept of "The Devil" can represent our darkest thoughts—the whispers of anger, envy, and self-destruction hidden in us. When we're tempted by harmful choices, we empower our inner devil. This part of us thrives on our weaknesses and wants to lead us astray. But we have the power to resist, to choose goodness and self-control over impulsive decisions.

Bad choices don't happen without warning. Often, we sense when we're about to cross a line. Our conscience speaks to us, sending signals through feelings of guilt and discomfort. Listening to these signals can prevent us from making mistakes we'll regret. It's a reminder that we always have choices. Drugs, alcohol, and other destructive habits may reduce the pain temporarily, but they give empower the devil within. Real strength lies in facing our struggles without losing ourselves to temptation.

People often seek relief in substances because they feel overwhelmed or broken. But these habits only mask the real issues. Choosing a different path, one that respects our well-being and inner peace, requires courage, but leads to genuine healing. The journey to overcome addiction or bad habits isn't easy, but it's possible. Each time we resist the temptation, we weaken the hold of our inner demons. The goal is to replace these destructive habits with healthy, constructive ones, empowering ourselves to live more fulfilling lives.

ADAPTING TO CHALLENGES

Life's unpredictability means that the ability to adapt is one of the most valuable skills one can develop. Adaptability doesn't mean suppressing our initial reactions to hardship, instead, its about learning to recalibrate our approach when confronting new challenges. Those who can shift gears, think creatively, and find alternative solutions, are often the ones to thrive under pressure. Imagine an entrepreneur whose business faces unexpected hurdles; by adapting, they might pivot their strategy, find new markets, or innovate products. Adaptation fuels resilience and enables personal and professional growth.

Adaptability also requires flexibility in our thinking and the willingness to entertain different perspectives. Often, our first instinct is to resist change, clinging to old ways despite knowing the inevitable. However, embracing adaptability can transform an obstacle into a stepping-stone. Maintaining an open mind leads to creating room for growth and innovation, paving the way for progress in the face of adversity.

GRATIFICATION AND GROWTH

Life rewards aren't handed to us; they're earned through hard work, resilience, and persistence. Each accomplishment represents the sum of our efforts and sacrifices, a testament to our strength and determination. Gratification doesn't come from shortcuts but from the satisfaction of achieving something meaningful. When we invest time and effort into our goals, the outcome feels truly rewarding.

There's power in perseverance. Many of history's greatest achievements were born from failure, not instant success. Thomas Edison, who failed countless times before perfecting the lightbulb, serves as a timeless example. Each setback taught him something new, bringing him closer to his goal. Similarly, every challenge we face has something to teach us, helping us grow stronger and wiser.

Gratification also comes from personal growth. Overcoming adversity helps us build resilience and self-confidence. The lessons we learn from our struggles shape who we become. Instead of fearing challenges, embrace them as opportunities for growth. Every small step forward, every hard-earned achievement, adds value to our lives. We become not just survivors but thrivers.

THE REALITY OF DISAPPOINTMENT

Disappointment is inevitable; life rarely gives us everything we want. But often, what seems like a setback is simply redirection. Many of our dreams may not be realized the way we envisioned, but sometimes, life has something better in store. Coping with disappointment is a valuable skill that helps us build resilience. Each time we face rejection or failure, we gain insight, preparing us for future opportunities.

Instead of dwelling on what we didn't achieve, we can focus on what's possible. A missed opportunity may open the door to something more fulfilling. Disappointment can be a teacher, guiding us toward paths that closely align with our true selves. If we view each setback as a stepping stone, we will find ourselves growing stronger with each experience.

Faith can be a source of comfort during times of disappointment. Believing that there's a greater plan that challenges serve a purpose, can help us navigate difficult times. Trust that, in time, things will fall into place. And remember, even in disappointment, there's often a lesson—a chance to grow and become better.

THE IMPORTANCE OF MENTAL HEALTH

Mental health is as vital as physical health, yet it's often neglected. Many of us carry invisible burdens, feeling isolated in our struggles. Talking about mental health isn't a sign of weakness; it's an act of courage. By acknowledging our challenges, we open the door to healing and growth. The stigma surrounding mental health is fading, but there's still work to be done. We must support each other, creating an environment where people feel safe discussing their struggles.

Life's demands can take a toll on our mental well-being, leading to anxiety, depression, and burnout. Recognizing the signs early can prevent these issues from worsening. Just as we seek help for physical ailments, we should feel comfortable seeking help for mental health. Reaching out can be the first step toward recovery.

Mental health resources are becoming more accessible, but many still feel alone in their struggles. Remember, help is available. If you're struggling, don't hesitate to reach out. Whether it's through friends, family, or professionals, support is out there. No one has to face their battles alone.

SUICIDE AND HOPE

The topic of suicide is often shrouded in silence, but it's a conversation worth discussing. Many people feel trapped in their thoughts, believing there's no way out. But every day offers a new chance—a new "what if." If you are having suicidal thoughts, know that there are people who care, even if you overlook them momentarily. Reaching out for help brings clarity, revealing options you hadn't considered.

Life is full of "what ifs." Don't let a moment of despair rob you of the chance to explore them. Every day you're alive, you have the opportunity to change your path. Even when hope feels distant, it's never truly gone. Allow yourself to believe that things can get better. This belief can be the foundation for building a brighter future.

THE POWER OF GRATITUDE AND REFLECTION:

Each day of life is a gift. Gratitude reminds us of the beauty in life's simple moments—the warmth of sunlight, the kindness of a friend, and the laughter of loved ones. Even in dark times, there's something to be grateful for. Reflecting on these blessings can shift our focus from what we lack to what we have, fostering a sense of peace and contentment.

Gratitude doesn't erase our struggles but helps us see them in perspective. When we appreciate life's small joys, we build resilience. We learn to weather storms with grace, knowing that each challenge is temporary. Reflect on what you're grateful for, and you'll find strength in unexpected places.

ROAD RAGE AND THE IMPORTANCE OF SELF-CONTROL

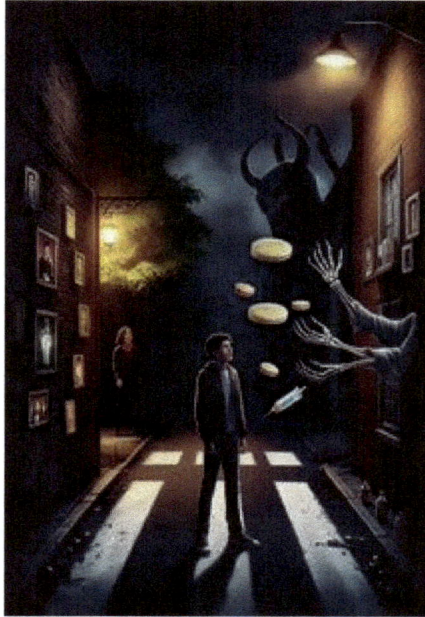

In moments of anger, it's easy to lose control. Road rage is a prime example. A minor inconvenience can quickly escalate, fueled by frustration and stress. But in these moments, we have a choice. Reacting with anger only adds fuel to the fire. Instead, breathe deeply and remind yourself that no inconvenience is worth compromising your peace.

Practicing patience can prevent minor annoyances from turning into major conflicts. When we control our reactions, we maintain our inner peace. The next time you feel anger rising, pause and consider the consequences. By choosing calm over chaos, you're not just avoiding conflict—you're nurturing your well-being.

THE JOURNEY TOWARD A MEANINGFUL LIFE

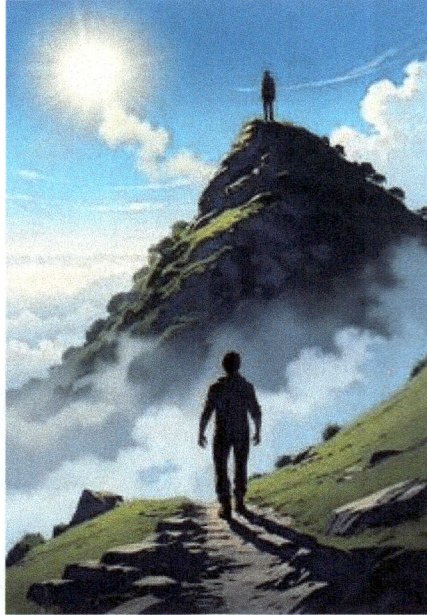

Life is full of choices. Each decision shapes who we are and who might become. Embracing our struggles, choosing kindness, and working toward our goals bring meaning to our lives. Each day is a new opportunity to be a little better, to learn a little more, and to make a positive difference.

Life's journey isn't always easy, but it's worth it. Embrace each moment, good or bad, as part of your story. Make choices that align with your values, and bring you closer to your goals. Remember, the journey itself is as important as the destination. Let each step bring you closer to becoming the best version of yourself.

EMBRACING UNCERTAINTY:

Uncertainty is a fundamental aspect of life. No matter how well we plan, some variables will always be beyond our control. Learning to find comfort within this uncertainty can be liberating. It frees us from the need to have all the answers and allows us to focus on the present. Embracing uncertainty requires trust—not just in ourselves but in the process. It's about cultivating faith that, despite the unknown, we possess the strength to handle whatever comes our way.

Consider a traveler exploring unfamiliar terrain. Without a map, they must rely on intuition, adapt to unexpected obstacles, and remain vigilant. This journey, though uncertain, builds confidence, resourcefulness, and courage. Life is similar; by embracing the unknown, we open ourselves to new experiences and personal growth. Uncertainty, instead of fear, is an invitation to learn and discover our capacity for resilience.

BUILDING INNER STRENGTH

Inner strength is the foundation that supports us in times of hardship. It isn't about suppressing emotion or pretending to be invulnerable but rather about maintaining a core of calm and assurance within. Building inner strength often begins with small acts of self-care and mindfulness. Each moment we choose to respond with patience rather than react impulsively, we fortify our resilience.

Inner strength is also nurtured by our values and beliefs. When we stay true to what we believe is right, we create a sense of purpose that bolsters us in challenging times. Think of inner strength as a wellspring from which we draw in difficult moments. By cultivating habits that nourish our minds and bodies—whether through meditation, exercise, or creative expression—we deepen this wellspring, preparing ourselves to face life's trials with courage.

CULTIVATING GRATITUDE:

Gratitude is more than a simple "thank you." It's an active practice of recognizing the abundance around us, even in difficult times. By focusing on what we have rather than what we lack, gratitude becomes a transformative tool, shifting our perspective to appreciation and positivity. In a culture that appreciates achievement, it's easy to overlook the small, consistent joys that make life beautiful.

Gratitude is powerful because it rewires our brain to notice positivity. When we appreciate small acts—share a meal, or a kind word—we learn to see life as full rather than scarce. This shift not only uplifts our mood but also strengthens our relationships, as others feel valued when we express genuine appreciation. During hardship, gratitude becomes a grounding force, reminding us that despite challenges, there is always something to be thankful for.

THE ROLE OF COMMUNITY

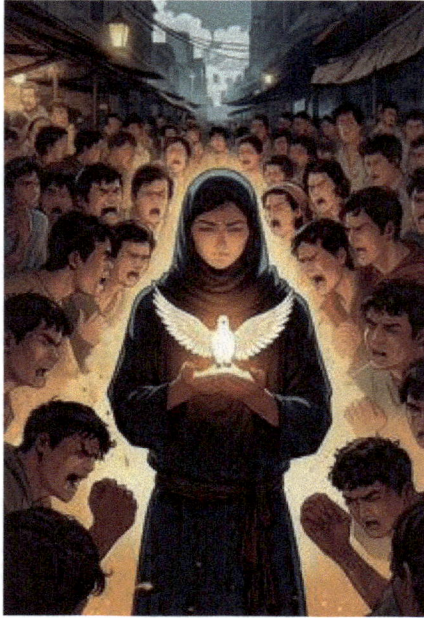

Human beings are inherently social creatures, and community plays a pivotal role in our lives. In times of crisis, our relationships offer us the support we need to heal, rebuild, and find hope. Being part of a community provides a sense of belonging and shared purpose that helps alleviate loneliness and fear. Friends, family, and mentors become our support systems, offering advice, encouragement, and sometimes just a listening ear.

Participating in a community also gives us a sense of agency. By contributing our time, skills, or resources, we not only help others but also reinforce our sense of worth. Think about the strength of communities that come together after natural disasters; each person's effort, no matter how small, adds to the collective resilience. In this way, community doesn't just support individuals—it amplifies their strength, making it possible to face even the greatest challenges together.

FOSTERING A SENSE OF PURPOSE

Purpose provides direction and meaning, grounding us in times of uncertainty. It doesn't have to be grand or world-changing; a sense of purpose can be as simple as caring for loved ones, pursuing personal growth, or contributing positively to society. By identifying what truly matters to us, we create a roadmap for our actions and decisions, encouraging us to pursue our goals.

Purpose is what fuels the spirit to persist when obstacles arise. Consider an artist who creates despite criticism or setbacks. Their purpose is self-expression, which sustains them through challenges. Similarly, when we pursue our sense of purpose, we likely stay motivated and resilient. Purpose gives us the strength to overcome hardship, reminding us that our actions contribute to something larger than ourselves.

NAVIGATING CHANGE AND UNCERTAINTY:

Navigating change when it's unexpected, is one of life's most difficult tasks. It often requires a shift in mindset—from seeing change as a disruption to viewing it as a new chapter filled with potential. Embracing this perspective isn't always easy, but by breaking down change into manageable steps, we allow ourselves to move forward, even when the path seems unclear. Each small action becomes a building block toward adaptation, helping us focus less on the fear of the unknown and more on the immediate, achievable steps in front of us.

Imagine someone facing a major career shift or relocation. This change might initially feel overwhelming, but by focusing on setting up a new routine, meeting new people, and establishing familiar habits in the new setting, they create a sense of stability amid the transition. Over time, these small, consistent steps turn what once seemed like a disruption into an opportunity for growth. By embracing this process, we cultivate the courage to handle other changes more confidently, building resilience with each new experience.

THE ART OF LETTING GO: Letting go can be as simple as releasing a grudge or as complex as forgiving someone for past mistakes. It's about recognizing that clinging to specific emotions, expectations, or relationships often hinders us more than it helps. Holding on tightly can keep us stuck, while letting go creates the mental and emotional space to welcome new possibilities.

Consider someone holding onto a past disappointment—a friendship that ended unexpectedly or a missed opportunity. Rather than dwelling on what could have been, practicing the art of letting go means allowing ourselves to heal and move on without resentment. Letting go is ultimately an act of self-liberation, freeing us from the grip of past emotions so we can embrace the present with a lighter heart.

CULTIVATING PATIENCE:

In a fast-paced world, patience is an essential skill essential for true growth. Patience facilitates reaching our goals with perseverance, even when immediate results are nowhere in sight. It's about trusting the process and understanding that worthwhile achievements often require time and consistent effort.

Consider a gardener who plants seeds in spring. They water and care for the soil, even though the plants are not yet visible. The gardener trusts that, with time, the seeds will sprout and eventually bloom. This same principle applies to any personal or professional goal. Patience involves nurturing our aspirations with persistent care, even when we can't yet see the outcome. Through patience, we learn to appreciate the journey rather than rushing toward the destination, allowing growth to occur naturally and meaningfully.

FACING FEAR: Fear is a powerful sentiment that often holds us back from taking risks or pursuing dreams. Facing fear requires a combination of courage, self-compassion, and, most importantly, a willingness to step into discomfort. Rather than avoiding fear, confronting it head-on can be transformative, helping us discover strengths we never knew we had.

Taking small steps, like practicing in front of friends or volunteering for minor speaking opportunities, gradually builds confidence. Each step makes the fear feel more manageable, transforming it from a roadblock into a growth opportunity. Facing fear is about knowing that discomfort is temporary and act of courage helps us grow stronger. Over time, we learn that fear is often an illusion—a mental barrier that loses power when confronted with resilience and determination.

THE POWER OF MINDFULNESS:

Mindfulness is the practice of being present in the moment, fully aware of our thoughts, feelings, and surroundings without judgment. This awareness brings clarity, helping us navigate life's challenges with a calm mind. By grounding ourselves in the present, mindfulness prevents us from regrets about the past or anxieties about the future.

A practical way to practice mindfulness is by starting each day with a simple breathing exercise or a few moments of meditation. By focusing on our breath, we anchor ourselves in the present, creating a sense of calm that we can carry into the rest of the day. Another mindful practice is to bring full attention to daily activities—whether it's enjoying a meal or taking a walk in nature. These small moments of presence help us cultivate a peaceful mindset, even amid life's noise, and bring a sense of calm that supports emotional resilience.

FOSTERING CREATIVITY: Creativity isn't limited to artists or writers; it's a powerful tool that we all can use to solve problems and express ourselves. By fostering creativity, we open up new ways of thinking and find unique solutions to challenges. Creativity gives us the flexibility to adapt, find joy in self-expression, and approach life with curiosity rather than rigid expectations.

Encouraging creativity could be as simple as trying a new hobby, exploring a different perspective on a familiar problem, or allowing ourselves to brainstorm without judgment. When faced with a challenge, approaching it creatively means asking "what if?" and considering solutions that lie outside traditional boundaries. For example, a team dealing with a work setback could use creative brainstorming techniques to come up with innovative solutions. Creativity becomes a source of resilience, allowing us to approach problems from new angles and discover untapped potential.

DEVELOPING SELF-COMPASSION:

Self-compassion means treating ourselves with the same kindness and understanding that we would extend to a friend. It's recognizing our imperfections without harsh self-judgment, allowing us to learn and grow from our mistakes rather than becoming discouraged by them.

Self-compassion nurtures resilience by fostering a safe inner environment where we can heal and thrive.

Imagine someone who has made a mistake at work. Instead of harshly criticizing themselves, they practice self-compassion by acknowledging the mistake, learning from it, and forgiving themselves. This approach doesn't diminish accountability but rather supports constructive growth. Self-compassion is essential for resilience because it empowers us to recover from setbacks with gentleness, making it easier to face future challenges with courage.

THE IMPORTANCE OF HUMILITY: Humility is a grounding quality that reminds us of our interconnectedness with others. It's about recognizing our strengths and achievements without overestimating our significance. Humility allows us to remain open to learning, admitting when we don't have all the answers, and valuing the perspectives and contributions of others.

Consider a leader who listens to their team's feedback with respect, recognizing that everyone has something valuable to contribute. This humility creates a collaborative atmosphere that fosters trust and innovation. In personal growth, humility keeps us grounded, preventing us from becoming complacent or prideful. It allows us to embrace each experience as a chance to learn, becoming better equipped to face life's challenges with wisdom and grace.

PERSISTENCE AND DETERMINATION: Persistence is the ability to keep moving forward, even when progress feels slow or the journey becomes difficult. Determination is what fuels that persistence, providing the inner drive needed to pursue our goals despite obstacles. Together, persistence and determination form a powerful combination that supports us in achieving long-term success.

Imagine an athlete training for a marathon. They might encounter setbacks, exhaustion, or moments of self-doubt, but their determination keeps them committed to their goal. Each day of training, no matter how small the progress, contributes to the bigger picture. Persistence is not about making giant leaps but about consistently showing up. Over time, the cumulative effect of these efforts leads to accomplishment, proving that success often lies in our ability to persevere, even when the journey feels endless.

FINDING MEANING IN ADVERSITY:

Adversity must be avoided, but it's a powerful teacher. By finding meaning in adversity, we transform hardships into valuable lessons that contribute to our growth. This doesn't mean dismissing the pain of difficult experiences, rather finding a way to learn and evolve from them.

Consider someone experiencing a challenging breakup. While the pain is real, it is best to focus on things to look for in future relationships, and grow emotionally. Adversity becomes a catalyst for self-discovery, helping us redefine our values, strengthen our character, and build resilience.

By reframing challenges as learning experiences, we create a mindset to help us endure tough times and emerge stronger.

BETTER HELP

The site www.betterhelp.com from one of my favorite shows on YouTube, Mr. Ballen. John B. Allen used to be in the Seal Team U.S. Navy; after he left the service, he said that he struggled going back to civilian life, and he found help through the services of better help through the comfort of your own home—anything help. Sometimes, what we thought was a hopeless case? It wasn't.

-1-800-suicide (784-2433)

-veterans crisis line 1-800-273-8255 (press 1)

-vets4warriors: 1-885-838-8255

-TTY: 1-888-262-7848

-FOH4You.com

-www.QPRinstitute.com

How can I help someone who is suicidal? Use ACE:

-Ask the question, "Are you thinking of killing or hurting yourself? Or do you think you might hurt yourself?

-Care, listen with compassion, voice your concern, be non-judgmental, and remove any means that could be used for self-injury.

-Escort, escort the individual to receive professional help (go to the nearest emergency room, local employee assistance program counselor, or chaplain)

THE NOTICEABLE SIGNS OF SUICIDAL INTENTIONS:

-Direct statements about suicidal intent.

-Making preparations for death shortly.

-Having weapons around in combination with excessive drinking.

-Increased risk-taking behaviors that are obvious to others and cause concerns.

-Purposely withdrawal from friends and family.

-Giving away prized personal items.

SUBTLE SIGNS:

More hidden signs of suicide are not as apparent to other people; these include the following;

-Extreme loneliness

-Feelings of rejection

-Changes in personality

-Increasing frequent thoughts of death

-Acquiring a weapon

-Impaired decision-making

-Practicing the act

-Loss of clear thinking

-Rigidity and an inability to problem-solve

-Elevated anxiety

-Feelings of sadness and confusion

WHY WOULD SOMEONE WANT TO ATTEMPT SUICIDE?

How does someone reach a point where the only solution they see is suicide? Several factors influence the desire to end one's own life:

-High-stress levels

-Helplessness and hopelessness

-Life situations

It's one of the most heartbreaking questions we can ask ourselves: why does someone reach a point where they feel that the only solution to their pain is suicide? It can feel unfathomable, especially when that person may have seemed outwardly okay or appeared to have everything going for them. But the truth is, there are often many different factors that contribute to this decision. The struggle is invisible to others and often even to the person experiencing it. The following factors can play a significant role in someone's decision to attempt suicide:

High-stress levels: Over time, stress can accumulate and become unbearable. The weight of work pressures, financial difficulties, relationship struggles, and other life challenges can leave someone feeling overwhelmed. When a person feels like they are constantly fighting an uphill battle and can't find a way to relieve the pressure, they might begin to see suicide as a way to escape the stress that has built up.

Helplessness and hopelessness: Feeling powerless to change one's circumstances is a critical factor in suicidal thoughts. When someone perceives that there is no way out of their pain or that their situation will never improve, the despair can become all-consuming. Hopelessness robs a person of their will to fight, and they may start to believe that no matter what they do, they will never be happy again. They may feel that there is no point in continuing.

Life situations: A variety of life situations can contribute to feelings of despair. These may include the loss of a loved one, a breakup, unemployment, or a major life transition. Sometimes, a combination of circumstances can push someone to the brink, making them feel like the weight of everything is too much to carry. For those who have experienced trauma or abuse, these past experiences can add layers of pain that make life feel unbearable.

I MISS THEM:

I've had a few co-workers in the past who, on the surface, seemed like the last people you'd expect to take their own lives. They were always the life of the office, quick to make jokes, with smiles that seemed to brighten even the toughest days. Friendly, happy, and wonderful to be around, they seemed to have it all together. Deep inside, they were likely carrying burdens or struggles that no one knew about. I wish they had opened up to someone—anyone. Perhaps they felt that they couldn't share their pain, or maybe they feared judgment or misunderstanding. I wish they had trusted me enough to share their burdens so I could have told them that everything would be alright. I would have told them that they mattered, that they weren't alone, and that I would have supported them, no matter what.

Now, all I have left are the memories. The empty desks, the unfinished projects, and the haunting silence that echoes in the spaces they once filled. I miss them deeply, and the loss cuts deeper with each passing day. It's hard to accept that we'll never share another laugh, never again hear their voice offering words of encouragement or wisdom. I hope wherever they are, they have found peace, but it's a peace that feels hollow for those of us left behind. There is a hole in my heart that can never be filled.

You know that saying, "God does not give us problems that we cannot solve," I believe that with all my heart. I'm not going to lie. Growing up, I didn't; I blamed god. Why? Why me? How could this happen to me? Am I really such a bad person? Why am I here? Why do I even exist? So many questions lingered in my mind. Growing older, I began to understand the answers. Now, I realize that I need to change my mindset—from negative thinking to positive thinking, from darkness to light. That's the best way I can describe it. My old thoughts simply weren't serving me anymore. I couldn't remember the day my thoughts awakened. Still, I do remember that one day, I was praying and said, "Lord, creator of heaven and earth and all things in the universe, I surrender my life to you," and ever since then, I felt that uplifting burden off my chest, I gave my absolute trust to my god and let my god guide me, I never felt so free.

That was the shift I needed—to transform my mindset from negativity to positivity, from darkness to light. It wasn't a change that happened overnight, but it made all the difference. My old way of thinking no longer served me—the doubts about my worth, my future, and my purpose. I can't pinpoint the exact moment my thoughts began to shift, but I remember the pivotal one. I was sitting quietly in my room, praying, when I said, "Lord, Creator of heaven and earth and all things in the universe, I surrender my life to You." In that moment, it felt as though the weight of the world lifted off my shoulders, finally released. I placed my trust entirely in my faith, in my God, and since then, I've felt freer than I ever imagined possible.

FACING THE UNKNOWN

As I reflect on the times that pushed me to my limits, I can't help but think about how many people feel alone in their struggles. We live in a world that, on the surface, may seem bustling with connections and relationships, but on a deeper level, many of us walk alone. It's not necessarily because we want to, but because the world sometimes demands it. There's an expectation that we always have to have it together, that we should be strong, and that we shouldn't show any vulnerability. Yet, this very expectation is what leads to so much internal conflict. When we don't feel safe enough to express our weaknesses or our struggles, we bottle everything up, keeping our fears and uncertainties in the dark corners of our hearts.

The truth is, life is messy. We can't always control our emotions or predict how we will react to the challenges life throws at us. But what we can control is how we respond when things get hard. I've learned that allowing myself to feel—really feel—what I'm going through is the first step in healing. It's okay not to be okay. For so long, I fought against my feelings, thinking that acknowledging them would make me weak or unworthy. But embracing those feelings, even the difficult ones, has been transformative.

It wasn't always easy to do this, and in fact, it took a long time for me to open up to others to let them see the cracks in my armor. I remember the first time I reached out to someone and said, "I'm struggling. I need help." It felt like a mountain of shame I had to climb, and I wasn't sure if I could do it. But the moment I said those words, I felt a shift. It wasn't an instant fix, but it was a breakthrough. That was the beginning of learning to trust others and trust myself. I realized that asking for help didn't make me weak—it made me human. We all need support sometimes, and acknowledging that we can't do it alone is one of the most powerful things we can do for ourselves.

There are days when I still struggle when I wake up feeling weighed down by everything on my plate, unsure of how I'm going to make it through the day. Those days don't happen as often anymore, but they still occur. However, I've learned not to fear them. I now see them as moments for growth. I can sit with those emotions, acknowledge them, and allow myself to experience them. It's all part of the process, and as painful as it can be, it's also an opportunity for deeper self-understanding. When we allow ourselves to be vulnerable, we open the door to healing. And healing, though slow, is always worth the effort.

I also realized that healing isn't linear. It's not a straight path, and it's certainly not a quick one. There are days when I feel like I'm taking two steps forward and one step back. And that's okay. It's okay to have setbacks. In fact, setbacks can be some of the most profound teachers. They teach us patience and resilience. They remind us that we are stronger than we think. No matter how many times I falter, I know that as long as I get up and try again, I'm making progress.

Sometimes, we need to let go of the idea of perfection. I've had to come to terms with the fact that I'm not going to get everything right every time. I've had to let go of the belief that I need to meet others' expectations or even my own. Life isn't about getting everything perfect. It's about showing up, doing our best, and continuing to move forward with compassion toward ourselves.

THE POWER OF COMMUNITY:

One of the most surprising discoveries I made along my journey was the profound impact of community. For so long, I could navigate everything on my own. I isolated myself, convinced that no one could truly understand what I was going through. But when I finally opened up, I realized how many people had gone through similar experiences; others were facing their own battles in silence.

It's easy to feel like we're alone in our struggles. We might look around at others and see them smiling, going about their lives, and we wonder why it feels like everyone else has it all together. But the truth is, everyone is carrying something—some weight, some burden. Some people are just better at hiding it than others. When we open ourselves up to others, we realize that we're not as alone as we think. In fact, we are all walking this journey together. There is power in sharing our stories finding those who understand us, and support us. Community is a balm for the soul.

Being part of a community doesn't mean that everything gets fixed immediately. It doesn't mean that the pain goes away or that the challenges disappear. What it does mean is that we don't have to face those challenges alone. We can lean on others, ask for help, and receive love and encouragement in the midst of our struggles. A strong community can be the difference between surviving and thriving. It provides a sense of belonging and support that we can't always find elsewhere.

I've found my community in unexpected places. Some of it has come from friends I've known for years, and some has come from people I've met along the way—people who share their stories of pain and growth, who offer a listening ear and a kind word when I need it most. I've learned that community isn't just about being around others; it's about being open to them, about allowing them to see the real, unpolished version of ourselves. When we let our guard down and allow others to do the same, we create space for healing and growth. We begin to realize that we are stronger together than we are apart.

LEARNING TO LET GO:

Another aspect of my journey has been learning to let go. Letting go of past hurts, of toxic relationships, of the need to control everything. For years, I clung to the idea that I had to hold on tightly to everything in my life. I thought that if I could control everything, then I could protect myself from pain. But I've learned that control is an illusion. No matter how much we try to hold on, there are things beyond our control. The key is learning to release the things that no longer serve us to trust that letting go is an act of strength, not weakness.

It's hard to let go of things that have been a part of our lives for so long. Whether it's a relationship, a job, or a dream, letting go can feel like losing a part of ourselves. But in reality, letting go is often the first step toward making space for something new. By releasing the things that are holding us back, we make room for new opportunities, new experiences, and new relationships. Letting go allows us to grow to become the person we are meant to be.

I've had to let go of a lot over the years—old hurts, grudges, and fears. I've had to let go of relationships that no longer served me of ideas about who I thought I should be. It's been painful at times, but it's also been liberating. The more I let go, the more I find peace. I've learned that sometimes, the best thing we can do for ourselves is to release what no longer fits. When we do, we make space for growth, healing, and renewal.

THE LIGHT WITHIN:

As I look back on my journey, I realize that there is a light within each of us—an inner strength, a resilience that we often forget exists. This light might get dimmed by life's challenges, by pain, or by fear, but it's always there. Sometimes, it just takes a little time for us to recognize it. It's easy to get caught up in the darkness, to focus only on the struggles and obstacles. But the light is always there, even in the darkest times. We just have to believe in it.

I've come to understand that this light is not something external. It's not something that others can give us; it's something that resides deep inside. It's the strength to keep going, even when it feels impossible. It's the will to rise above the pain and continue moving forward. This light doesn't always shine brightly. Sometimes, it flickers, dimming in response to the storms we face. But it's always there, waiting for us to reach out to it, to reignite it, to let it guide us through the tough times.

The key is to trust in it, to know that we have what it takes to face whatever comes our way. Life will always throw challenges in our direction, but we don't have to face them alone. And we certainly don't have to face them in darkness. We have the power to find light within ourselves, to create hope, and to keep moving forward, one step at a time.

Quote: FIRST, OPEN YOUR HEART, THEN YOUR MIND, BEFORE YOU SEE

I started reading and listening to audiobooks; I highly recommend the book "The Power of Positive Thinking" by Doctor Allan Peal. I've also been listening to the book and audiobook of "The Secret." For the past four years, I've immersed myself in it, playing audiobooks while driving to and from work and during my breaks whenever I can. This experience has helped me truly embrace the ideas presented in the book and forget my old, negative thinking patterns in favor of a more positive mindset. Things are looking up after I switched my negative thoughts to positive thoughts; I really couldn't have turned my life around if I hadn't changed. You might wonder how I know this will work. Well, the truth is, you don't. It comes down to a word called "faith"—believing in something you can't see. That's where the phrase "leap of faith" comes from. Consider it this way: if we could see the future, we'd all be rich by now. The reality is we can't know what tomorrow holds. We get up each morning ready to face a new day and do our best. Then comes the night, and we thank god for another safe and wonderful day. Every day, we see homeless people and war in the news from other parts of the world. People are dying senselessly. Everything they own is gone, and people are still fighting to live their lives despite incurable diseases such as cancer. I'm grateful every day, even in the face of my problems and body aches. But when I look at what others are going through, I realize that my struggles are insignificant compared to their suffering. Because of this, I find it hard to complain about the little things in life.

I started reading and listening to audiobooks a few years ago, and it has truly changed the way I think about life. One of the first books I came across was *The Power of Positive Thinking* by Dr. Norman Vincent Peale. This book had a profound impact on my life, and I highly recommend it to anyone who is struggling with negative thought patterns. I also found *The Secret*, both in the book and audiobook format, to be an invaluable resource in understanding how the law of attraction works. For the past four years, I've immersed myself in these teachings, listening to audiobooks on my way to and from work, as well as during my lunch breaks whenever I can. Over time, these teachings have helped me truly embrace the idea that we are the creators of our own destiny.

I've learned to let go of the old, limiting beliefs that once held me back. There was a time when my mind was consumed by doubt and negativity, and I found it difficult to break free from that cycle. But as I began to fill my mind with positive thoughts, my perspective on life started to shift. Gradually, I stopped seeing the world as an enemy and began seeing it as a space full of opportunities, growth, and change. Things are definitely looking up for me since making that shift. I truly believe that I would not have been able to turn my life around if I hadn't first transformed my way of thinking.

You might wonder how I can be so certain that this approach works. And the truth is, you don't always know right away. The journey of self-improvement requires faith—faith in yourself, in your efforts, and in the process. Faith is essentially believing in something you cannot see, trusting that good things will come even when you can't yet grasp how or when. This is why the term "leap of faith" exists. Think about it: if we could see the future and know what would happen, we would have no reason to fear or doubt. But life is not like that. We can't predict tomorrow, but we can choose how we show up today. And that choice, that act of showing up, is powerful.

When I wake up each morning, I remind myself to face the day with the belief that it can be a good one, regardless of what challenges arise. When the day ends, I thank God for giving me another opportunity to live, learn, and grow. I've become increasingly aware of how fortunate I am, especially when I see the suffering that others around the world endure. The news is full of stories about war, homelessness, and disease—people losing their homes, their families, and even their lives. Despite all of that, they find the strength to push forward. And it is in these moments that I stop complaining about my own problems. Sure, life is hard at times, and we all go through rough patches. But in comparison to the global suffering that exists, I find it hard to focus on my own struggles without a sense of gratitude.

BORN:

Some of us are born rich, while others are born poor; we can't change that. However, we can change who we are right now. By transforming ourselves, we can become whoever we want to be. It starts with looking in the mirror and asking yourself some important questions about how to improve. Better physically, in health, and in attitude? Sometimes, we forget simple things in life: to "Ask." We can ask our family or friends to research online or visit the library. There are so many ways to find an answer. The answer is Out there.

Sometimes, we have a mental breakdown, and sometimes, that person loses it. We are human, and when those moments arise, it's crucial to take a deep breath, regain your composure, and ask yourself, "What am I doing?" This is my way of waking myself up when I find myself caught up in something negative or feeling angry over a person or situation. It works every time; it prevents me from causing more harm or escalating the situation due to impulse.

If you're feeling down, I highly recommend listening to some motivational speakers. There was a time when I felt like my life was going in circles as if I were going nowhere. I would wake up in the morning, go to work, and then return home, repeating the same routine day after day. I realized I had to break this cycle, and one day, I simply told myself that I was tired of feeling tired.

No doubt about it: life can be challenging; when hard times come, "stop" and think, and say it to yourself in comparison to what is happening to some person on the other side of the planet…… my problems are nothing compared to what they are dealing with, but yet they get up and fight for another day, no house no job, nothing just their selves and their family hoping for another day, because another day is hope. I sometimes find myself feeling sorry for my problems, but I pray and hold onto the hope and faith that tomorrow will be better.

I often reflect on the struggles of others and wonder if my misery is worse than theirs. When I compare my situation, I realize that mine isn't so bad after all. I suppose I'm just trying to improve my inner self, but ultimately, I still have to face my own challenges. I am not trying to make light of other people's misery; I am just saying that I am grateful for everything I have despite my circumstances.

Yes, life can be challenging and often complicated, but that's life sometimes; it's how you face the problems and issues, big or small. The problem is that we deal with them and then move on.

I guess I'm in my point of life where I am amazed by how much you can achieve in life by working hard to achieve what you want in life; I am just a simple man with simple needs, and the little things I have means a lot to me I am happy, not yet content to that point I believe I still have a long ways to go, but that's the good thing about life that it's constant it allows you to be better every day as long as we are giving our life a chance, I always say to myself I maybe down but not out. So, I move on with that faith in my heart and mind.

Some of us are born into wealth, while others are born into poverty. The circumstances of our birth are beyond our control, but that doesn't mean we are doomed to remain in that place forever. We are not defined by where we start; we are defined by where we choose to go. It's all about personal transformation. The power to change is within each of us. But the first step is to acknowledge where we are now and ask ourselves some critical questions: How can I become better, stronger, and more capable? How can I improve my physical health? How can I transform my mindset so it aligns with my highest aspirations?

Sometimes, we forget that the answers to these questions are out there, waiting for us to discover them. Whether it's asking a mentor, researching online, or visiting a local library, there are so many resources available to help us find the answers we need. All we have to do is ask. And yet, at times, we find ourselves facing breakdowns— mental, emotional, or physical. We feel overwhelmed, and in those moments, it's crucial to pause, take a deep breath, and ask ourselves, "What am I doing?" This question is a wake-up call, a chance to stop ourselves from spiraling further into negativity or impulse. It's about taking control of our thoughts and emotions rather than letting them control us.

There was a time when I felt like my life was stuck in a repetitive cycle. I would wake up, go to work, come home, sleep, and repeat. Every day felt the same. I realized that I had become so accustomed to this routine that I no longer questioned it. But one day, something shifted inside me. I got tired of feeling tired. I got tired of going through the motions without any sense of purpose or progress. I decided that I couldn't let another day pass without making a change. I chose to break the cycle. And let me tell you, that decision was one of the best choices I've ever made.

When times get tough, it's easy to focus solely on our own problems. But sometimes, it helps to stop and reflect on what others are going through. We hear about people in war-torn countries facing the unimaginable: no home, no security, no food, no healthcare. Yet, they continue to fight for their survival. They have no guarantee of tomorrow, but they continue to hope. When I think of them, it makes me realize how much I take for granted. Even when I am struggling, I have a roof over my head, food to eat, and people who care about me. I have the opportunity to make a difference in my own life and in the lives of others.

There have been times when I felt like my problems were insurmountable. But when I take a step back and compare my struggles to the hardships of others, I realize that my situation isn't as bad as it seems. I am still here. I am still breathing. I still have the chance to grow, to improve, and to change. And so, I hold on to that hope, that faith, that tomorrow will be a better day.

Yes, life can be hard. There will always be obstacles, big and small. But the key to navigating life's challenges is not to avoid them but to face them head-on. Life isn't about being perfect; it's about how we handle imperfections and setbacks. It's about perseverance and resilience. Every time I encounter a setback, I remind myself that it's not the end—it's just part of the journey.

Quote: EMBRACE LIFE AS IF THERE IS NO TOMORROW

When one issue is resolved, another often takes its place. Does that mean life is synonymous with problems? It can certainly feel that way, but what truly matters is how we face them. Whether big or small, problems will always exist, but I choose to confront them head-on.

As I grow older, I've discovered countless ways to tackle challenges. Sometimes the solution is immediate, and other times it takes longer—but there's always a way forward. You'd be surprised at the possibilities when you approach each problem with determination and an open mind.

It often feels like the problems in our lives never cease, doesn't it? Just when you think you've resolved one issue, another one appears on the horizon. It's almost as if there's no escape from the cycle of challenges that we face daily. As I think about that last sentence, I find myself wondering: is life synonymous with problems? For a long time, it felt that way to me. It seems that no matter how hard we try to maintain balance or peace, life throws curveballs at us. The truth is, it's not just the problems that define our lives. It's how we approach them, how we respond, and how we grow from them. Life is a series of moments—some good, some bad, but all of them contribute to who we become. In a way, problems aren't the enemy. How we deal with them is what shapes us.

Come to think of it, the body itself is full of problems. It might be something as small as a headache or as big as an illness, but does it matter how we face these physical challenges? At the end of the day, it's still a problem, but how we approach it—whether with fear or with resilience—determine whether it defines us. I choose to confront problems head-on. Sure, there are moments when it feels overwhelming, but as I grow older, I discover new ways to tackle these challenges. Sometimes, a solution presents itself immediately, but there are also times when it might take days, weeks, or even longer to find clarity. Through it all, there are always ways to address issues, even when they seem insurmountable at first. Believe me, you'll be amazed at the possibilities if you give yourself the chance to explore them.

Our bodies are intricate machines, constantly at work to keep us alive and functioning. They digest food, pump blood, repair cells, and respond to stimuli—all without us consciously thinking about it. But for all its miraculous design, the body is also frail, vulnerable, and prone to issues. From the moment we are born, we face a lifetime of problems in the form of physical ailments, accidents, and limitations. The older we get, the more aware we become of these challenges. We might start with a simple sprained ankle, a common cold, or a temporary fatigue, but eventually, our bodies begin to slow down. We age, we weaken, and we become ill. The inevitability of physical decline can feel overwhelming at times, especially when we are confronted with our own limitations. And yet, despite the problems our bodies bring, they are also a source of incredible strength.

When we experience pain or sickness, it often feels like the end of the world. We begin to question our mortality, to wonder how much longer we have before our bodies break down entirely. But there is also a profound resilience within the body—a resilience that can surprise us. It's amazing how, even after an injury or illness, we can often heal and recover, often more quickly than we expect. The body is constantly working to repair itself, to restore balance, and to heal. This is a metaphor for life itself: we face challenges, setbacks, and obstacles, but we also possess the strength to overcome them. It may not always be easy or immediate, but with time, we can heal, grow, and emerge stronger than before.

What's more, the body teaches us about impermanence. It reminds us that nothing lasts forever—not our physical strength, not our youth, not our health. And yet, in its fragility, the body also invites us to take better care of ourselves, to appreciate what we have, and to honor the vessel that carries us through this life. We might not always have control over our physical state, but we do have control over how we care for ourselves how we nourish and tend to our bodies. This care, this reverence for our physical form, becomes a way of honoring our life's journey. Even as we age and our bodies change, we learn to adapt, to accept, and to move forward with grace.

Not all humans are imperfect. Now, you might be wondering why I would say that. In a world where we often see the worst of humanity—wars, crimes, hatred—can we really say that there is goodness left in people? Should I lose hope in humanity because of the terrible things some people do to others? No, of course not. Despite the darkness, there is always light. As there is terrible, there is also good. Over the years, I've come to realize that there will always be a balance of good and evil, light and dark. They are two sides of the same coin. I often find myself reflecting on whether there could ever be a place in the universe without either of them. A world with no darkness, where all is light? Or a place where only darkness exists and no light ever breaks through? It's an intriguing thought and one that leads me to wonder if life as we know it depends on the existence of both.

This thought process makes me wonder about other forms of life in the universe. Aliens—if they exist—would they face the same struggles and issues we do here on Earth? What drives them to explore the galaxies? Would they still be searching for answers if they lived in a place without conflict, without problems? What if they are driven by the same questions we face daily, just in different forms? It's a thought that sparks curiosity. After all, if we can relate to one another through our shared experience of problem-solving and growth, then surely other life forms—if they exist—have their own struggles to contend with. Perhaps we all have our own battles, no matter where we come from.

Life is an intricate tapestry of joy and sorrow, of triumph and failure, of moments so fleeting we barely have time to grasp them before they slip away. When we speak of living as if there is no tomorrow, we acknowledge the inherent transience of existence. It's not about throwing caution to the wind, nor is it about recklessness. Rather, it's an understanding that we don't know how long we have in this world. The days can blend into one another with such quiet monotony that we forget they're finite, that every single moment is precious. We get caught up in the routine of "going through the motions"—work, chores, obligations—believing that time is infinite. But it is not. Time is the most precious commodity we have, and it's the one thing we can never get back once it's gone.

So, we must choose to embrace life fully, to take risks, to love deeply, to experience joy with abandon. If we truly live as though there is no tomorrow, we learn to cherish every instant—whether that means savoring a quiet morning cup of coffee, engaging in meaningful conversation, or simply sitting in stillness with our thoughts. When we stop taking time for granted, we begin to appreciate life in all its messy, beautiful complexity. The moments of peace become just as significant as the moments of chaos. The mundane is no longer mundane—it is simply life unfolding as it should.

One might think that such an approach could lead to anxiety, to a fear of loss. But in truth, it brings a deep sense of liberation. If you accept that tomorrow is not guaranteed, you can shed the burden of expectation, the fear of missing out and live in the now. For in the now, there is no past to regret and no future to dread. There is only this breath, this heartbeat, this precious moment that exists solely for you to experience.

Living with this mindset requires a deep-seated trust in yourself and in the universe, as well as the courage to make bold choices. The first step might feel like a leap into the unknown, but as you navigate the unknown, you'll realize that the world is full of opportunities waiting to be seized. Even the seemingly small decisions—the way you respond to a situation, the energy you put into your relationships, or the way you approach your work—hold immense power. How we choose to engage with the world in any given moment defines not just our present but also our future.

The idea of human imperfection is one that has been passed down through generations, reinforced by religion, philosophy, and cultural norms. And while it's true that no one is without flaws, I believe that there is beauty in our imperfections. Perhaps the true essence of humanity is not in our perfection but in our ability to learn, to grow, and to evolve. We make mistakes, we fall short, but these experiences teach us invaluable lessons. The mistakes we make are not signs of failure; rather, they are opportunities for growth. It's through our errors that we learn empathy, humility, and resilience. It's when we stumble that we discover the strength to rise again.

But beyond that, there are those rare individuals who seem to transcend the limitations of human imperfection. These are the people who inspire us, who seem to embody wisdom, compassion, and grace. They are the ones who, despite their own struggles, choose to lift others up.

They see the good in the world even when it feels like there's little to find. In their presence, we are reminded that it is possible to live a life of integrity, kindness, and purpose. These individuals aren't perfect—they, too, face challenges and imperfections—but they have learned how to navigate them with strength and poise. They teach us that perfection is not the goal; living authentically is.

I think this is why we are often drawn to stories of people who overcome adversity and rise above their circumstances to do something remarkable. These stories resonate with us because they mirror the potential we all have within us to rise above our flaws to strive for greatness in spite of our limitations. They remind us that we don't have to be perfect to make a difference. Our imperfections are what make us human, and it is through embracing these imperfections that we can create meaningful connections, find purpose, and experience growth.

GOD TAKES CARE OF EVERYTHING:

The question is, why do people still commit suicide? Your answer is as good as mine because we can all do such an act. I say this because the quality of life—whether good or bad—depends on perspective. For some, living in a small house feels terrible, while for others, a larger house represents a better life. However, it's important to recognize that each of us has different standards and values when it comes to what constitutes a fulfilling life. I think we don't have to live like the Joneses. You can live the comfortable lives that you want to live.

I want to share one of my favorite bible verses, Philippians 4:13, which means, "I can do all things through him who strengthens me." I am not religious, but this verse came to me when I needed it most; I have problems left and right, and I don't know where else to go or what to do. Whenever I face challenges in my life, I find myself repeating the phrase, "I can do all things through Him who strengthens me." This reminder helps me stay focused and resilient.

Occasionally, singing can help us forget the problem momentarily, allowing the mind to divert for a while. Though that's not a permanent solution to the problem, but for a minute, it would make your problem go away. It resets our thoughts, letting us regroup our thoughts and refresh our focus on the problem.

Why does life or death matter to us as humans? For me, its simple—I care about living for loved ones as much as for myself. From a young age, I believed my life wasn't mine alone—it equally belonged to the people around me. That belief shaped my purpose. I've always tried to live selflessly. Even though we have only one life, I choose to dedicate it to making a difference for others. I see this life as a bridge, a transition to whatever comes next. I believe my deeds in this life will shape the life waiting for me beyond this one, whether it's good or bad. I often wonder if living a good, meaningful life will lead to something better, while wrongdoing could result in a worse fate.

An old saying goes—bad deeds lead to hell. Maybe there's some truth in that—who knows? It's a concept that makes me pause and think about the inequalities in life. Why are some born wealthy while others into poverty? Could it be tied to the lives they've lived before? The idea resonates with me, even if it's just a possibility. Do I believe in death? Absolutely. Death is inevitable, but how we live before we die is all that matters. If we can spread kindness and help the world become a better place, then our lives are worth it. That's the core of what I believe wholeheartedly.

Suicide is one of the most tragic and difficult topics to confront, yet it is something that touches so many lives. It's a question that I've asked myself more times than I care to admit—why would someone decide that their pain is so unbearable that they would choose to end their own life? The reasons are complex, and every story is different. For some, the burden of depression, grief, or mental illness becomes so overwhelming that they feel there is no other way out. For others, the weight of shame, rejection, or loneliness drives them to the edge.

Ultimately, it's the feeling of being trapped, of not seeing a way out that leads people to this devastating decision.

When we talk about suicide, it's essential to approach the subject with compassion and understanding. We can't fully comprehend the pain that someone who is contemplating suicide feels, but we can try to offer support and empathy. One of the greatest challenges in this world is the stigma surrounding mental health, the idea that we should be able to "snap out of it" or "just think positive." But mental illness is not something that can be willed away. It's a real and serious condition that affects millions of people worldwide. For those who are struggling, it often feels like there is no hope left.

I think the key to understanding why some people might choose suicide lies in the absence of hope. When we lose sight of hope, when we feel disconnected from others, and when we don't see a way forward, life can feel impossible to navigate. It's in these moments that we need to remind each other that we are not alone. That there is hope, even when it doesn't feel like it. That there is always the possibility for change, for healing, for a new beginning.

Mental health is just as important as physical health, and we must work to create a world where it is okay to seek help where we can talk openly about our struggles without fear of judgment. We must strive to be there for one another in our darkest moments, to listen without judgment, and to offer the love and support that can make all the difference.

Time heals all wounds

I agree with that statement 100%. When we lose someone, we feel the world has collapsed/fallen on us, that there is no tomorrow. We sometimes ask ourselves, what is the purpose of living? What is the purpose of life that someone we love so much has passed on? Sometimes, we find ourselves staring at nothingness as if all hopes are gone, and the will to live is gone. All of this often runs through our minds. Just like a scar on our skin that tells a story from the past, it's just that—a scar, a memory, a reminder. We must move on; as humans, we shouldn't dwell on the past since we cannot change it. Time is the greatest teacher of all. Instead, let's enjoy the present, look forward to the future, and learn from our history. This is a phrase we've all heard at one point or another, often when we're struggling with pain or loss. When we lose someone we love, when we go through a difficult breakup, or when we experience deep grief, it can feel as though we will never recover. The wounds feel so deep, and the pain so raw that we can't imagine a future without it. Over time, the intensity of the pain lessens. The edges of the wound become less jagged, and eventually, we are able to move forward, even if we never truly forget. Time doesn't erase the memories or the love, but it gives us the space to heal. It allows us to process our emotions and come to terms with our loss.

This doesn't mean that we won't experience pain again in the future, but it does mean that the pain we feel today will not last forever. Time offers us the gift of perspective. It allows us to look back on our experiences with greater clarity and to see how much we've grown. What once felt like an insurmountable obstacle becomes a stepping stone on the path to healing and personal growth.

The passage of time doesn't just heal wounds; it also provides us with the opportunity to reconnect with our sense of purpose, to rediscover what brings us joy, and to move forward with a renewed sense of hope. We are all capable of healing. With time, patience, and self-compassion, we can mend the wounds that life inflicts upon us and emerge stronger, wiser, and more resilient than before.

It's a saying that I wholeheartedly agree with. When we lose someone, it feels as though the entire world has collapsed. It can feel like there is no tomorrow, that there's no reason to go on. We ask ourselves, what is the purpose of living when someone we love is no longer here? In those moments, the pain is so raw and intense that it can be hard to imagine a future without that person. Sometimes, we find ourselves staring at nothing, feeling as though hope has vanished and the will to live is gone. But, just like a scar on our skin—a mark of something that happened in the past—our wounds, too, will heal with time. They become reminders, not of the pain, but of the strength we found in overcoming it.

We shouldn't dwell on the past because we cannot change it. Time is the greatest teacher of all, and through its passage, we learn to accept, to heal, and to move forward. Instead of holding onto past grief or regret, we can focus on the present and the future. Even when it feels like everything is falling apart, there's always the possibility of renewal, of finding peace again. Life moves forward, even when we feel stuck. And with time, we will find our way back to joy, back to meaning, and back to living fully again.

That brings me to a question that weighs heavily on my mind: Why do people still commit suicide? It's a heartbreaking thought and one that doesn't have an easy answer. I think we all grapple with such questions at some point. Why is it that some people feel so hopeless, so overwhelmed by life, that they believe the only option is to end it all? Your answer might be as good as mine because, in reality, we all have the capacity to make such a choice. It's a sobering truth. The quality of life—whether good or bad—often comes down to perspective. For some, living in a modest house feels like a burden, while for others, the same space represents a sense of contentment. Similarly, the pursuit of wealth, status, or power can either be a source of joy or an endless chase that never satisfies. Our values and our perspectives determine how we navigate the world, and it's essential to recognize that everyone's journey is different.

That's why I believe we shouldn't live our lives trying to keep up with others. You don't have to live like the Joneses. You can choose to live a life that feels comfortable and fulfilling for you. What works for someone else might not work for you, and that's okay. The key is to find your own path, your own way of living that brings peace and contentment. It's about understanding that you don't need to measure your success by external standards but by the fulfillment and purpose you create for yourself.

One of my favorite Bible verses is Philippians 4:13: "I can do all things through Him who strengthens me." Now, I'm not religious in the traditional sense, but this verse came to me at a time when I needed it most. There were days when I felt completely overwhelmed by the challenges in my life. When everything seemed to be going wrong, and I couldn't see a way out, this verse was a reminder that strength is not something we have to find within ourselves alone. Sometimes, it's about tapping into something greater than us—whether that's God, the universe, or simply the power of our own will to keep moving forward. This verse helped me stay focused and resilient when life seemed impossible. Whenever I face challenges now, I repeat the phrase: "I can do all things through Him who strengthens me." It's a mantra that keeps me grounded.

Sometimes, when we find ourselves struggling, it might help to do something small and seemingly insignificant—like singing a song or walking in nature. I know it doesn't solve the problem right away, but for that moment, it provides a mental reset. A distraction, maybe. But a necessary one. It reminds us that not every moment is defined by the weight of our problems. We can always shift our focus, even if just for a short time, to something that brings us joy or peace. And in that shift, we might find new energy and perspective to face what's ahead. Sometimes, it takes a little creativity or a change in focus to reset our minds and push through.

When I was younger, I believed my life didn't belong solely to me. It belongs to the people around me. This sense of responsibility shaped the way I lived my life. I strive to be unselfish to live with purpose. I believe that my actions impact the world around me, and that's what gives my life meaning. Yes, I may have only one life to live, but I choose to dedicate it to others, to leave something behind that matters. It's not always easy, and there are times when I question whether what I'm doing makes a difference. But I continue because I believe in the idea that this life is a bridge—a journey that will carry me to whatever comes next. The choices I make now, the actions I take today, will shape whatever follows. I often wonder if doing good in this life will lead to a better next life while doing wrong might result in something worse. There's a saying that if you live a bad life, you'll end up in hell. Whether or not you believe in hell doesn't matter. What matters is the impact of your actions. We all wonder why some people are born into wealth while others live in poverty. But perhaps the answer lies in how we live, in the choices we make each day.

As a child, I believed my life wasn't just for me—it belonged to everyone around me. I saw myself as part of a greater whole, and this sense of responsibility shaped how I approached every day. I made decisions based on the idea that my actions affected others. The thought that my life could have a meaningful impact on the world was what motivated me. I believed in living for something greater, for a cause, and I found purpose in that.

As a grown up, I've realized that I only have one life to live, and I've chosen to dedicate it to the people I care about. This isn't always simple, and sometimes I question whether what I do truly matters. There are moments when I wonder if I'm making the right choices or if my efforts are in vain. But I continue, even in uncertainty, because I believe that every action count. Even the smallest of efforts have value, even if the impact isn't always immediately clear.

To me, life is a journey—a series of steps that take us forward, with each decision creating a path for the future. I like to think of it as a bridge, where every choice builds toward something greater, not just for me, but for the people around me. I often wonder if living a life full of compassion and integrity leads to something better after we pass, or if our wrongdoings lead us somewhere worse.

Some people believe that living a sinful life results in eternal punishment. I'm not focused on the idea of punishment, but on the consequences of our actions in this world. It makes me think about why some are born into privilege and others struggle. It could be that our actions, not just our circumstances, shape our destiny. What we choose to do each day—the way we treat others, the kindness we offer—can influence the life we live.

Death is something everyone faces, and I accept it as an inevitable part of the human experience. But the way we live our lives is what gives meaning to the inevitable end. I don't think the value of a person's life is measured by wealth or status. It's about the connections we make, the love we share, and the ways we touch others' lives.

Imagine if everyone focused more on how to improve the world around them than on what they could take from it. The world would look very different, I believe. We would see fewer selfish acts and more kindness. I choose to be a part of that change. My goal is to leave behind something positive, something that continues to impact the world long after I'm gone. The good we do creates ripples, spreading through time and space, impacting lives in ways we may never fully understand.

We all have the ability to make a difference. I want to be part of the solution, not the problem. By living with intention, by caring for others, and by making the world a better place, I believe we can all leave a legacy worth remembering. My hope is that the kindness we give, no matter how small, will continue to shape the world for generations to come.

Yes, I believe in death. We all die eventually. It's an inescapable truth. But how we live our lives matters. The legacy we leave behind is not in the things we accumulate or the status we achieve. It's in the relationships we build, the kindness we show, and the difference we make in the lives of others. We have the power to shape the world around us, and that is what I choose to focus on. Let's spread good in this life and leave this world a better place than we found it. I genuinely believe that in my heart and mind.

QUOTE: YOU LIVE YOUR LIFE FROM THE CHOICES THAT YOU MAKE.

Every day, I wake up and say in my prayer, "Thank you, Lord, for a wonderful evening and for giving us sleep so we may face today with strength and energy." I also pray, "Thank you, oh Lord, for this wonderful day we are about to receive. Please guide us and protect us. Thank you."

QUOTE: MILLIONS OF PEOPLE AROUND THE WORLD WILL GIVE THEIR ARMS AND LEGS TO WHAT YOU HAVE RIGHT NOW; BE GRATEFUL.

ADDICTION

Addiction, in its various forms, is a struggle that affects millions of people worldwide. It is not merely about the addiction to a substance or behavior—it is a deep, multifaceted issue that involves both physical and mental components. While the external consequences of addiction are often visible, the internal battles that individuals face can be even more debilitating. These internal struggles may include feelings of guilt, shame, isolation, and worthlessness, all of which contribute to the perpetuation of the addiction itself. The cycle of addiction can create a false sense of control, which ultimately reinforces the compulsive behaviors that drive people further away from recovery.

The beginning of an addiction often stems from a person trying to manage stress or emotional turmoil. Initially, these coping mechanisms may offer a sense of relief, whether it be through alcohol, drugs, food, or even work. However, over time, these short-term relief strategies turn into long-term dependencies, and what was once a temporary solution becomes the primary means of survival. People who struggle with addiction often feel caught in a paradox: they may feel the need to use substances or engage in addictive behaviors to cope, but those very behaviors also contribute to the problems they are trying to escape from. The longer the cycle continues, the harder it becomes to break free.

Substance Use Disorder and Its Impact on Mental Health

One of the most widely recognized forms of addiction is substance use disorder (SUD), which involves the compulsive use of substances like alcohol, drugs, or prescription medications. While SUD is classified as a mental health disorder, its effects are far-reaching, impacting not only the individual's emotional and physical well-being but also their relationships, social standing, and overall quality of life. People with substance use disorder often experience a distorted perception of reality. The compulsive urge to use the substance overrides the person's logical reasoning and decision-making abilities, leading them to prioritize the substance over everything else.

When an individual engages in substance abuse, their brain chemistry is altered. Neurotransmitters responsible for feelings of pleasure, such as dopamine and serotonin, are affected by the drugs or alcohol, making it difficult for the person to experience natural pleasure from everyday activities. This chemical imbalance contributes to the cycle of addiction—when an individual attempts to quit or reduce their use, they often experience withdrawal symptoms that are both physically and mentally distressing. The withdrawal process can trigger anxiety, irritability, fatigue, and even more severe symptoms such as seizures or hallucinations. For many, the fear of withdrawal makes it harder to quit, even when they recognize the negative impact the addiction is having on their life.

Additionally, addiction often goes hand in hand with co-occurring mental health disorders, which complicate the situation even further. It is common for individuals with substance use disorder to also suffer from depression, anxiety, post-traumatic stress disorder (PTSD), or other psychiatric conditions. In some cases, substance abuse may begin as an attempt to self-medicate the symptoms of these underlying disorders. For example, someone with anxiety may begin drinking alcohol to calm their nerves, but over time, the reliance on alcohol to cope becomes an addiction. The relationship between addiction and mental health is complex and bidirectional—while addiction can lead to the development of mental health issues, mental health issues can also make someone more vulnerable to developing an addiction.

The Role of Genetics and Environment in Addiction

There is no single cause for addiction. Rather, it is the result of a combination of genetic, environmental, and psychological factors. Research has shown that genetics play a significant role in determining an individual's susceptibility to addiction. Certain genes may predispose individuals to be more likely to develop an addiction, whether it be to alcohol, drugs, or other substances. However, genetic predisposition does not guarantee that someone will develop an addiction—it only increases their risk. Environmental factors, such as childhood trauma, stress, or exposure to addiction in the family, can also contribute to the development of substance abuse problems.

For example, children who grow up in households where addiction is prevalent may be more likely to develop similar behaviors as adults. This could be due to modeling behavior, where children unconsciously learn to cope with stress and emotions through substance use. Additionally, childhood trauma, such as physical or emotional abuse, can have long-lasting effects on a person's mental health and can lead to the development of maladaptive coping mechanisms, including addiction.

The environment plays an equally important role in addiction. Factors such as social circles, peer pressure, socioeconomic status, and access to substances can influence the likelihood of someone developing an addiction. For example, individuals living in communities with high levels of substance abuse or poverty may be more likely to experiment with drugs or alcohol. Peer pressure, particularly during adolescence, can also make it harder for individuals to resist substance use. When addiction is normalized within certain social groups, it can feel almost inevitable for individuals to follow suit.

The Psychological Toll of Addiction

Beyond the physical consequences, addiction takes a significant toll on mental and emotional health. People who are addicted to substances or behaviors often experience feelings of isolation and loneliness. As the addiction worsens, individuals may withdraw from social activities, relationships, and even family members, further exacerbating feelings of alienation. They may feel disconnected from those who do not share their struggles, which creates a sense of "us versus them." This isolation can lead to feelings of hopelessness and despair, making it even harder to break free from the addiction.

Guilt and shame also play a central role in the psychological toll of addiction. Many individuals struggling with addiction experience a deep sense of shame about their behavior, particularly if it has led them to hurt others or damage their relationships. This shame often leads to more substance use, as individuals attempt to numb the emotional pain caused by their actions. Ironically, the more they try to numb the feelings of guilt and shame, the more they perpetuate the cycle of addiction.

Self-esteem is another critical component that is often undermined by addiction. People who struggle with substance abuse or addictive behaviors often feel worthless or incapable of change. Their sense of self-worth becomes tied to their addiction, and they may believe they are undeserving of a better life. This negative self-image reinforces the belief that they are powerless to change and that recovery is impossible.

Treatment and Recovery: The Road to Healing

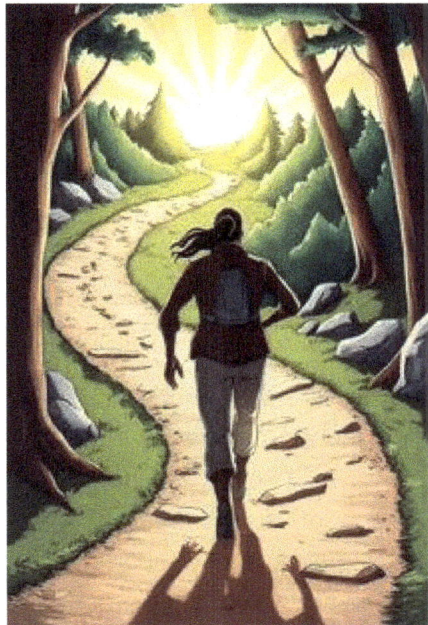

While therapy, medical intervention, and support groups form the backbone of recovery, one of the most powerful and often overlooked aspects of healing from addiction is the support system. Having a network of friends, family, and professionals who understand the challenges of addiction can make all the difference in overcoming it. Recovery is not a solitary journey—it's one that requires the compassion, understanding, and commitment of those around the individual.

Friends and family often play a pivotal role in the recovery process, but they, too, need to be educated about addiction and its complexities. Without a clear understanding of addiction's psychological, emotional, and physical effects, it can be easy for loved ones to unintentionally contribute to the individual's struggles. In fact, enabling behaviors—such as giving in to a person's requests for money or covering up for them—can exacerbate the addiction rather than help. It is essential for family members to learn how to set boundaries, offer constructive support, and encourage their loved one to stay committed to recovery.

Some families also choose to participate in therapy sessions together. Family therapy can help break down barriers of communication, rebuild trust, and address any unresolved issues that may have contributed to the addiction. It is common for addiction to create dysfunction in family relationships, and without addressing these issues, recovery can be much more difficult. Family therapy provides an opportunity to heal as a unit, rather than as individuals isolated in their pain.

The role of friends is just as important. Often, people in recovery may feel isolated or misunderstood, and having a group of friends who offer genuine support can create a sense of belonging. These friends may also serve as a source of accountability, keeping the individual grounded in their commitment to stay sober. It's essential for people in recovery to find individuals who are also focused on their own well-being, as this creates a positive, nurturing environment that fosters growth.

While loved ones are essential, professional support is equally important. Addiction specialists, counselors, and therapists provide expert guidance in navigating the emotional and psychological aspects of recovery. They help individuals recognize the underlying causes of their addiction, such as trauma, stress, or mental health disorders. By addressing the root causes, recovery can move beyond merely abstaining from the addictive behavior and toward a more comprehensive approach to healing.

One of the key aspects of professional treatment is the use of evidence-based therapies, such as cognitive-behavioral therapy (CBT) and dialectical behavior therapy (DBT). These therapies help individuals change their thought patterns and emotional responses to stress and triggers, making it easier to resist the temptation of returning to old behaviors. CBT, for instance, teaches individuals how to identify and challenge negative thought patterns, while DBT helps individuals cope with intense emotions and find healthier ways to regulate their reactions. Both therapies have proven highly effective in addiction treatment and are commonly used in inpatient and outpatient programs.

Another essential part of treatment involves addressing co-occurring mental health disorders. As mentioned earlier, many individuals with addiction also struggle with conditions such as depression, anxiety, PTSD, or bipolar disorder. Without addressing these mental health issues, addiction treatment is unlikely to be effective. Integrated treatment programs that address both addiction and mental health simultaneously have been shown to improve outcomes for individuals with co-occurring disorders. For example, a person with depression may not fully benefit from addiction treatment until their depressive symptoms are managed. Addressing both aspects at the same time allows for a more holistic and lasting recovery.

Breaking free from addiction is a difficult journey, but it is possible with the right support, resources, and mindset. Recovery is not a linear process—it is full of ups and downs, setbacks and breakthroughs.

However, with perseverance and the right tools, individuals can achieve lasting recovery and lead fulfilling lives.

One of the first steps in the recovery process is recognizing the need for help. Admitting that there is a problem is often the most difficult part of the journey. Many people with addiction live in denial or minimize their struggles, believing that they can control their behaviors on their own. However, once an individual acknowledges their addiction, they can begin to explore treatment options and take steps toward healing.

The most effective treatments for addiction typically involve a combination of therapy, medical intervention, and support from others. Therapy can help individuals understand the root causes of their addiction and develop healthier coping mechanisms. Cognitive-behavioral therapy (CBT), for example, is a common form of therapy used to help individuals reframe negative thought patterns and behaviors associated with addiction. Through CBT, individuals learn to identify triggers, manage cravings, and cope with stress in healthier ways.

In some cases, medical treatment may be necessary to manage withdrawal symptoms and stabilize the individual physically. This may involve detoxification programs, where individuals are monitored as they go through the withdrawal process. Medication-assisted treatment (MAT) is another option for individuals with substance use disorder. MAT uses medication to help reduce cravings and withdrawal symptoms, making it easier for individuals to remain abstinent.

Support groups, such as Alcoholics Anonymous (AA), Narcotics Anonymous (NA), and other 12-step programs, are also invaluable in the recovery process. These groups provide individuals with a sense of community and understanding, as well as a safe space to share their experiences. The support from others who have walked the same path can be incredibly powerful, as it reminds individuals that they are not alone in their struggles.

Family therapy can also play a significant role in the recovery process, as addiction often affects not only the individual but also their loved ones. Through family therapy, families can learn how to support the individual in recovery and rebuild trust and communication. It can also help address any unresolved issues that may have contributed to the addiction in the first place.

In addition to traditional therapies and treatments, mindfulness practices have gained recognition as valuable tools in addiction recovery. Mindfulness refers to the practice of staying present in the moment without judgment. It encourages individuals to observe their thoughts, emotions, and physical sensations without becoming overwhelmed by them. This is particularly important in recovery because it helps individuals manage cravings, deal with stress, and reduce the likelihood of relapse.

Mindfulness can be practiced in many forms, including meditation, breathing exercises, or simply paying attention to one's environment with intention. Studies have shown that mindfulness-based interventions can be highly effective in reducing substance use and preventing relapse. Mindfulness helps individuals reconnect with their inner selves, which may have been neglected or suppressed during their years of addiction. By cultivating a sense of awareness and acceptance, individuals can learn to navigate the difficult emotions and situations that trigger their addictive behaviors.

Another related practice that is critical in recovery is self-compassion. Many people struggling with addiction have internalized negative beliefs about themselves, often as a result of shame and guilt surrounding their behaviors. These negative self-perceptions can make it difficult for individuals to move forward in their recovery, as they may feel unworthy of love or healing. Self-compassion involves treating oneself with the same kindness and understanding that one would offer to a friend. It allows individuals to acknowledge their mistakes without letting those mistakes define them. By practicing self-compassion, people in recovery can reduce the harsh self-judgment that often leads to relapse.

Self-compassion is not about excusing harmful behavior or shirking responsibility. Rather, it is about acknowledging that mistakes are part of being human and that healing takes time. Individuals who practice self-compassion are better equipped to accept the setbacks that occur in recovery and to persevere in the face of challenges. This shift in mindset is essential for long-term success in addiction recovery, as it helps individuals build resilience and emotional strength.

Understanding Setbacks and Building Resilience

One of the harsh realities of addiction recovery is that relapse is often part of the process. It is important to understand that relapse does not mean failure—it is simply a setback that can be overcome with the right mindset and support. Many individuals who have struggled with addiction experience multiple relapses before achieving lasting recovery. What matters is how one responds to these setbacks.

Resilience is key in overcoming addiction. People who are resilient are able to bounce back from setbacks, learn from their mistakes, and continue moving forward. Building resilience takes time and requires developing coping strategies to deal with stress, triggers, and cravings. It also involves cultivating a strong support system, practicing self-care, and setting realistic goals for the future.

Additionally, addressing underlying mental health issues is crucial for long-term recovery. Many individuals with addiction also suffer from mental health disorders, and treating these issues is essential for preventing relapse. For example, someone with depression may begin using substances as a form of self-medication. If the depression is not addressed, it may lead to further substance use in the future.

Addiction is a complex and challenging issue that impacts every aspect of a person's life. While the road to recovery can be long and difficult, it is not an impossible journey. With the right treatment, support, and mindset, individuals can break free from addiction and rebuild their lives. Healing is possible, and recovery is within reach. The key is to take the first step, ask for help, and believe in the possibility of a brighter future. Addiction may be a powerful force, but it is not stronger than the human capacity for resilience, healing, and change.

Recovery is not just about abstaining from addictive substances or behaviors; it is about creating a new life that is fulfilling and meaningful. For many individuals, part of the recovery process is developing a new sense of purpose and direction. This often involves setting goals, exploring new interests, and rebuilding relationships that may have been damaged during the period of addiction.

For those who have experienced addiction, the idea of living a fulfilling life without relying on substances or addictive behaviors may seem daunting. However, it is important to remember that recovery is an ongoing process. It is about taking small steps every day toward building a better future. Part of the process involves finding healthy, positive activities that can replace the time and energy that was once devoted to addiction. This may include hobbies, career goals, volunteer work, or new relationships. In many cases, people in recovery find that they are capable of achieving more than they ever thought possible, once the constraints of addiction are lifted.

Relapse prevention is another essential aspect of building a sustainable future in recovery. While relapse is common, it is not inevitable. The key is to develop a set of coping strategies to deal with triggers and stressors that could lead to a return to old habits. These strategies include practicing mindfulness, engaging in physical exercise, seeking professional support, and staying connected with loved ones. Developing a strong support system that provides encouragement and accountability is crucial for maintaining long-term sobriety.

Part of relapse prevention also involves learning how to recognize warning signs that could indicate a slip. For example, if a person begins to isolate themselves, neglect self-care, or feel overwhelmed by stress, these could be red flags that they need additional support. By staying vigilant and aware of these signs, individuals can take proactive steps to prevent relapse before it occurs.

I must have had depression in the past. Because I was drinking a lot, a lot, meaning I consume on my days off or whenever I'm off the following day. Or am I just an alcoholic? I didn't see a doctor about why I drink; that is why it was a question of whether I have depression or not. However, looking back, I don't think I'm an alcoholic because I did manage to kick that bad habit off. So, I think I had depression, if I'm to analyze myself, probably because of all the problems I was dealing with at that time. I brought up this topic because sometimes we do things we are not supposed to, but we do it anyway because we think it would solve our issues. Drinking doesn't solve anything; it only adds more problems to those we already face. Often, there are unseen health issues, particularly mental health problems, which aren't visible. You can't touch or feel them directly—though you certainly feel the effects of a hangover the next morning. Sometimes, our drinking can hurt our loved ones, others, and even ourselves.

I know there are other forms of addiction, but I'm only going to mention 3 in this topic: my thoughts on addiction; some people's definition of a person with addiction is using illegal drugs (substance abused) or alcohol, hence sight that is our perception or thoughts about people with an addiction, but for me the definition of people with an addiction a habit that can harm yourself and others (especially yourself) substance abused, alcohol are the two leading well-known addiction in the world, but not so much or seldom we talk about the food addiction, which for me should be the number one addiction in the world, let me explain, drugs and alcohol can break a family apart and can lead to crime to society that also leads you to incarceration, also can lead you to lose your mind then eventually leads to death. Food addiction leads to obesity, which leads to health scares such as diabetes, high cholesterol levels, and blood pressure, among others. It can also break the family apart (not always), but it can also cause depression, which leads to mental illness and eventually leads to death.

I wrote about this topic because, as I mentioned, it often goes unspoken. For example, when we see a homeless person on the street, we quickly label them as an alcoholic or drug user, possibly assuming they also have a mental illness. Yet, when we encounter someone who is overweight (not necessarily obese), we rarely say anything—even to our own family. We tend to remain silent, despite knowing that being overweight can lead to serious health issues like diabetes, high blood pressure, strokes, and even heart attacks. Food addiction, if not recognized, will lead you to your doctor to prescribe you medication, which is what often the doctor does prescribe all sorts of medication, which leads to relying on prescription medication. Food addiction is a slow death, while drugs And alcohol lead you to a much faster death. There Is a lot of help out there; recognize your self-issues; often, it's mental (usually, we don't admit it) that leads to physical health issues. Be open-minded when seeking professional help and also when you are doing your research. There is always an answer to a problem.

Telltales that there may be something wrong with ourselves; mental illness can include the following.

- I am feeling anxious or worried. Most people get worried or stressed from time to time.

- I am feeling depressed or unhappy.

- Emotional outbursts.

- Sleep problems.

- Weight or appetite changes.

- I am being quieter or more withdrawn than usual.

- Substance abuse.

- Feeling guilty or worthless.

- Changes in academic performance.

- Sex drive changes.

- Increased sensitivity.

- Nightmares.

- Relationship difficulties.

- Excessive worrying or fear.

- Feeling excessively sad or low.

- Confused thinking or problems concentrating and learning.

- Extreme mood changes, including uncontrollable "highs" or feelings of euphoria.

Four types of mental issues:

- Mood disorders (such as depression or bipolar disorder).

- Anxiety disorders.

- Personality disorders.

- Psychotic disorder (such as schizophrenia)

What causes mental health issues?

Drug and alcohol misuse or abuse, as well as domestic violence, bullying, and other forms of abuse in adulthood, can have profound and lasting effects on individuals. Significant trauma—such as military combat, surviving a life-threatening incident, or being a victim of violent crime—can also deeply impact mental health and overall well-being. These experiences often lead to a cycle of pain, isolation, and, in many cases, an increased risk of substance abuse as individuals seek ways to cope with their trauma. Addressing these issues requires awareness, support, and resources to help those affected heal and reclaim their lives.

Alcohol or other substance abuse problems, call the NATIONAL DRUG AND ALCOHOL THREATH referral routing service; 1-800-663-Help. Or 1-800-662-Help.

BORROWED TIME

If you think about it, this life is a borrowed time; although tomorrow is uncertain, we must try to better ourselves and others with what we can do now. Some of us want a reward for every good thing that we do. More than any material thing in this world is that fulfillment inside our heart; that invisible void inside ourselves gets filled whenever we help others. It doesn't have to be big or small; any act of kindness will do.

This reality reminds us that we are not invincible, nor are we immune to the passing of time. Every day we wake up is another opportunity, a chance to make the most of the time we have, to improve ourselves, and to better the lives of others. In a world that often rushes forward without pause, it's easy to get swept up in the demands of the moment and forget the preciousness of time. Yet, it's in these quiet moments of reflection that we begin to understand that what we do today matters—not just for ourselves but for those around us.

The notion of time being borrowed encourages a mindset of urgency. Not in the sense of rushing, but in the sense of recognizing the fragility of our existence and the importance of making each moment count. We can't control every aspect of life, but we can control how we respond, how we choose to act, and the values we prioritize. The world might not always reward us for our good deeds in ways we expect—sometimes the results are not immediately visible, and the gratitude we hope for doesn't always come. But that shouldn't deter us from continuing to do good.

Some of us live with the expectation that we should receive a reward for every positive thing we do. We help others, and we hope that somehow, we will be compensated, either materially or emotionally. In a society where success is often measured by wealth, status, or achievements, it can be easy to fall into this trap of transactional thinking. But the truth is that fulfillment doesn't come from external rewards—it comes from within. It's the sense of peace, contentment, and purpose that fills the empty spaces inside us when we do something meaningful, no matter how small it seems.

True fulfillment doesn't always come from grand gestures or monumental acts of kindness. In fact, sometimes it's the little things that have the most profound impact. Holding the door open for someone, offering a kind word when it's least expected, listening to a friend in need, or simply being present for someone who is going through a tough time—these small acts are powerful beyond measure. They might not make headlines or be celebrated on a grand scale, but they fill the invisible void within us, reminding us that we are capable of making a difference in the lives of others.

It's easy to underestimate the power of kindness. We often think that we need to do something grand to make a meaningful impact. But the truth is that kindness, no matter how seemingly insignificant, has a ripple effect. One small act of compassion can spark a chain reaction that spreads beyond our immediate reach. It can inspire someone else to do the same, creating a web of positive energy that weaves through our communities and the world at large. And in the process, it nourishes our own hearts, giving us a sense of connection and belonging in a world that can sometimes feel disconnected.

Sometimes, the most fulfilling moments are not the ones that come with applause or recognition but the quiet moments of satisfaction that come from knowing that you've done something good. It's the knowledge that your actions have made a difference in someone else's life, even if they will never be able to repay you. This sense of inner fulfillment is a powerful force—it transcends the need for material rewards and leaves behind a legacy of goodness that can never be taken away.

As we navigate through life, it's important to remember that every moment is an opportunity to do better. The mistakes we make, the missteps we take, are part of our journey, but they don't define us. What matters is how we choose to move forward, how we choose to respond to challenges, and how we choose to treat others. When we embrace the idea that life is borrowed time, we realize that each day is a gift—a chance to make the world a little better, even if it's just in a small way.

We don't know how much time we have, and that uncertainty can be both daunting and liberating. It can be easy to get bogged down in the weight of the unknown, to focus on what we don't have or what we've yet to accomplish. But the truth is, the time we have right now is all that matters. How we spend it, how we live in the present, and how we treat the people we encounter today—that is what truly counts.

In a world that often feels chaotic and unpredictable, the simple act of kindness is a constant. It is something that we can always control, no matter what else is going on around us. And when we give kindness, we also receive it. The beauty of human connection lies in our ability to support one another, to uplift those around us, and to share in each other's struggles and joys. In this shared experience, we find a sense of belonging and purpose that transcends time.

So, if you ever find yourself wondering whether your efforts matter, whether the kindness you offer is enough, remember this: every small act of goodness contributes to a larger picture. The time you have in this world is borrowed, yes—but how you use that time can leave a lasting impact. You don't need to wait for tomorrow to start making a difference. The power to shape your life and the lives of others is in your hands, right now.

Let your actions today be guided by love, compassion, and kindness. Do it not because you expect something in return, but because it fills the void within you and brings light to those around you. It is the only true reward that will remain long after time has passed.

It's also important to remember that the impact of kindness is not always immediately visible. Sometimes, we may never see the results of our actions, and that can make it hard to gauge whether our efforts are worth it. We may go through life giving, loving, and offering help, only to wonder if it has made any difference. But the truth is that the ripple effects of our actions often spread far beyond what we can see. A kind word, a listening ear, or a small act of generosity might inspire someone else to do the same. That person may, in turn, touch the lives of others, and the chain of goodwill can extend far beyond what we could ever know.

In this way, our actions, though small in the moment, accumulate over time, creating a broader shift in the world around us. Even when we cannot see the direct consequences of our kindness, we can trust that it matters. It may not be immediately obvious, but it is always powerful. We might never know the full extent of how our actions affect others, but we can trust that they do.

And while kindness is often a choice that comes from the heart, it's also something that we can cultivate intentionally. It's easy to fall into patterns of self-interest, to get caught up in our own struggles and desires. But if we step outside ourselves, even just for a moment, and look at the world through the lens of others, we can begin to see the immense power of a small act of kindness. Each day is an opportunity to practice compassion, to reach out to someone who may be hurting, or to lend a hand to someone who may need support. We don't have to wait for the perfect moment to act. The perfect moment is always right now.

The idea that life is borrowed time is a reminder of the impermanence of everything we experience. We often get caught up in the idea that we have all the time in the world, that tomorrow is guaranteed, and that we can always start later. But the reality is that time is finite. No one can predict how long he or she have, and that uncertainty makes every moment all the more precious. It's not about living in constant fear or anxiety about the future, but about being fully present in the moment we are given.

When we approach life with the understanding that time is limited, we are more likely to prioritize the things that truly matter—relationships, personal growth, and the well-being of others. We begin to see that material wealth, social status, and fleeting pleasures are not the things that will bring us lasting fulfillment. True fulfillment comes from the relationships we nurture, the love we give, and the difference we make in the lives of others.

This doesn't mean that we should neglect our personal goals or dreams. On the contrary, it's important to pursue the things that bring us joy, passion, and purpose. But in doing so, we should not lose sight of what is truly valuable: the connections we create and the impact we have on the world around us. If we spend all our time chasing external validation or accumulating things, we may miss out on the deeper, more meaningful aspects of life.

One of the key aspects of living with the awareness that our time is borrowed is the ability to practice gratitude. Gratitude allows us to appreciate the present moment, to find joy in the small things, and to recognize the value of the people and experiences in our lives. When we are grateful for what we have, we shift our focus away from what we lack, and we open ourselves to the richness of the world around us. Gratitude reminds us that even in the face of hardship or uncertainty, there is always something to be thankful for—whether it's the love of a friend, the beauty of nature, or the opportunity to help someone in need.

Moreover, living with borrowed time encourages us to embrace the unpredictable nature of life. We can't control when our time will come to an end, nor can we control every twist and turn that our journey takes. But we can control how we respond to those challenges. We can choose to meet adversity with grace, to face difficult situations with resilience, and to embrace change as an opportunity for growth. Life is not about avoiding hardship or running away from difficulties. It's about how we navigate them and how we choose to show up for ourselves and others, even when things are tough.

In many ways, the knowledge that life is borrowed time frees us from the pressure of perfection. We don't have to be flawless, and we don't have to have all the answers. We simply need to do our best with the time we have, to live with integrity, kindness, and a sense of purpose. It's not about being perfect—it's about being authentic, about showing up with love and compassion, and about making the most of the moments we are given.

As we reflect on the concept of borrowed time, we also recognize the importance of legacy. What will we leave behind when our time here is done? This is a question that can guide our choices and actions. Legacy isn't just about tangible achievements or material wealth. It's about the impact we have on others—the way we make people feel, the love we share, and the positive changes we bring to the world.

The way we live, the way we treat others, and the values we embody will be the lasting impressions we leave behind. It's the kindness we offer, the support we give, and the love we spread that will endure long after we are gone. Our legacy is built not on what we accumulate, but on how we make others feel and the mark we leave on their hearts.

Ultimately, the understanding that life is borrowed time challenges us to be intentional about how we live. We are reminded that each moment is a gift, and how we choose to spend that gift matters. It's not just about striving for personal success or accumulating wealth. It's about making a difference in the lives of others, about being present, about embracing the beauty of each day, and about living with purpose and gratitude.

When we view our time on earth as borrowed, we begin to see the preciousness of every moment. We realize that each day is an opportunity to live with intention, to practice kindness, and to make the world a better place. We understand that our time here is limited, and that makes it all the more important to make it count.

In the end, it's not the accolades, the possessions, or the achievements that will define our lives. It's the love we give, the kindness we show, and the difference we make in the world around us. Life is borrowed time, and it's up to each of us to make the most of the time we have.

I DARE YOU:

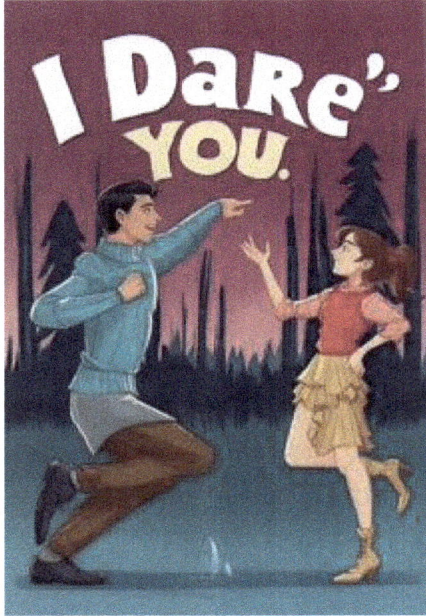

When I was much younger, I was told by the people around me that I could not do what I wanted to do, that I could not be creative, and that I was incapable of making things happen. I felt inadequate at the time. Hearing things like that as a child can severely impact your self-esteem, and I carried that feeling throughout my teenage years. Deep down, I knew I was capable and felt the need to prove myself. Although I lost many years believing a false narrative, I still held on to a sense of belief. So I didn't stop dreaming and still pursued what I wanted in life; all that I hoped for and wished for came true and more. Although sometimes we want something from God and don't get it, I understand why I didn't; we all play a role in this life. You may not get what you hope for, but he will reward you with something even better. I am now at the point where everything I had hoped for I got, and from this point in my life, I now have extras or bonuses. Believe that God works mysteriously; if you let him guide you, more significant things will happen. Work hard, think smart, be positive, stay in the light, and stay away from darkness; you have a choice. With God on your side, "I dare you, "tell yourself you could not do it.

Looking back, I see that there were times when I asked for things and didn't receive what I thought I wanted. But I now understand that there was a greater plan at work. There were reasons I didn't get certain things, and those reasons had to do with the bigger picture of my life. We all play a part in this grand story, and sometimes, we're not meant to have certain things because there's something better waiting for us, something that aligns more closely with who we're meant to be.

Life has a way of unfolding in ways we cannot predict, and while it's easy to become discouraged when things don't go as planned, I've learned that sometimes, what we think we want isn't what we need. God works in mysterious ways, and when we allow Him to guide us, He opens doors to things far greater than we could have imagined. At this point in my life, I've reached a place where everything I once hoped for has materialized, and along the way, I've been blessed with things I never even dreamed of. These are the "extras" or bonuses that come when we allow ourselves to trust the journey and have faith that everything happens for a reason.

I know there will be challenges ahead, but I now know that I am capable. My belief in myself has been rebuilt, and I've learned to trust that if I stay positive and continue to work hard, the path will continue to open before me. The journey hasn't been without its struggles, but I now see those struggles as lessons, as stepping stones that have led me to where I am today.

The key is to keep going, even when the road seems uncertain. The universe, or God, will always guide you to where you need to be, and when you let go of trying to control everything, you open yourself up to a bigger vision. There's something incredibly powerful about staying in the light, about keeping your energy aligned with positivity, and about not allowing darkness—whether it's doubt, fear, or negativity from others—to pull you off course.

We all have a choice in how we navigate this life. The journey may not always be easy, but when we trust in our purpose and believe that we are worthy of the dreams we have, we can accomplish incredible things. And with God by our side, there is nothing we cannot do. So, when those voices—inside your own head or from the world around you—tell you that you can't do it, I challenge you to look them in the face and say, "I dare you to tell me that again." Keep believing in yourself, keep trusting in the process, and keep moving forward. Because, with hard work, faith, and positivity, you will prove them wrong.

The journey toward realizing one's dreams can often feel like a long, winding road. Along the way, there are numerous obstacles that can challenge your confidence and make you question your worth. It's easy to become discouraged when things don't go according to plan or when people around you make you doubt your abilities. But I've learned that the obstacles are not the end—they're just part of the process. They are the experiences that teach you the most about yourself, your resilience, and your true potential.

When I look back on the times I struggled, I see now that they were necessary for my growth. Each setback was a lesson in disguise, each failure a stepping stone toward success. In those moments when I felt like giving up, I often found that it was the deepest sense of self-belief and inner strength that kept me going. It wasn't the external validation that made the difference—it was the quiet, unwavering confidence that no matter how hard it got, I was capable of overcoming it. I didn't always feel it in the moment, but I've come to realize that, in the end, the hardest moments are often the ones that shape us the most.

Belief in yourself is a powerful force. It's what pushes you to keep moving forward, even when everything around you seems to be falling apart. But belief is not always something that comes naturally, especially when you've spent so much time doubting your abilities or internalizing negative messages. It takes time to rebuild that belief, but it is possible. You don't need to have it all figured out right away. The important thing is to keep taking steps, even small ones, in the right direction. The fact that you're moving forward, even when it feels like you're not making progress, is enough. Each step adds up, and before you know it, you'll look back and realize how far you've come.

There will always be moments of doubt. There will always be people who try to discourage you or make you feel like your dreams are too big or too impossible. But those moments don't define you. What defines you is how you respond. Will you allow their doubts to seep into your soul, or will you choose to believe in the possibility of your own success? I've learned that success is not just about achieving a certain goal or reaching a specific destination. Success is about the journey itself. It's about showing up every day, even when it feels like you're not getting anywhere. It's about staying committed to the process, knowing that eventually, the hard work will pay off.

One thing I've come to understand is that success does not always come immediately. It doesn't come on a perfect timeline. Sometimes, you'll put in the work, do everything right, and still not see the results you expect. And that's okay. That's part of the journey. The key is to remain patient and trust that everything is unfolding exactly as it's meant to. If you keep showing up, keep doing the work, and keep believing in the process, eventually the rewards will come. But they won't always come in the form you expect. Sometimes, they'll come in ways that are more unexpected and even more fulfilling than what you had initially hoped for.

I remember a time when I was caught in a cycle of disappointment. I would work tirelessly toward a goal, only to fall short of it. It was disheartening, to say the least. But looking back, I realize that those moments were actually the most formative in my journey. They taught me resilience, perseverance, and the importance of staying committed even when things didn't go my way. Now, when I face challenges, I know that I can handle them. I know that I have the strength to keep moving forward, even if the path is not always clear.

Through it all, I've come to realize that our success is not determined solely by our achievements, but by our ability to persist through challenges. Our true strength lies in our ability to keep going, even when the going gets tough. Every time we pick ourselves up after a setback, we become stronger. Every time we overcome doubt and push through fear, we gain more confidence in ourselves. Every time we take action, even when we're unsure, we move closer to the life we want to create for ourselves.

But it's also important to remember that success isn't just about individual accomplishments. It's about how we show up for others, how we lift them up along the way. Life is not a competition; it's a journey we all take together. While it's important to pursue your own dreams and work hard to achieve them, it's equally important to be a source of support and encouragement for others. We're all in this together, and when we help others along the way, we create a community of people who are empowered to reach their fullest potential. Helping others doesn't take away from your own success— it adds to it. There's a special kind of fulfillment that comes from seeing someone else succeed because of the encouragement or guidance you've offered.

I've also learned that it's okay to ask for help. There's no shame in seeking guidance from others, whether it's a mentor, a friend, or a professional. Sometimes, we can't do it all on our own, and that's perfectly fine. It's okay to lean on others when we need it. There's strength in vulnerability, and there's power in surrounding yourself with people who believe in you and support your vision. We don't have to carry the weight of the world on our shoulders alone. We can share the load and walk the journey together.

Another important lesson I've learned is the power of gratitude. When things get tough, it's easy to focus on what's not going right, to dwell on the obstacles and the challenges. But taking time each day to reflect on what you're grateful for can completely shift your perspective. Gratitude has the power to turn any situation around. It reminds you of all the good things in your life and helps you to see that even in the midst of struggle, there is always something to be thankful for. When you shift your focus from what's going wrong to what's going right, you begin to attract more positivity into your life. Gratitude opens the door to abundance, and it allows you to see the beauty in even the smallest moments.

As I reflect on my own journey, I realize that every moment, every setback, and every victory has led me to where I am today. And I can't help but feel grateful for the lessons I've learned along the way. While the road has not always been easy, it has been worth every step. I've learned that success is not about the destination—it's about the person you become along the way. It's about the strength, resilience, and wisdom you gain from facing adversity and the compassion and empathy you develop from helping others.

I now know that I am capable of more than I ever imagined. I've proven to myself that no matter what others say or what challenges come my way, I am strong enough to overcome them. And most importantly, I've learned to trust the process, knowing that if I keep moving forward, keep believing, and keep working hard, the universe will meet me halfway. There's no limit to what can be achieved when you stay committed to your dreams, stay true to your purpose, and keep believing in the power of your own potential.

In the end, the most important thing is to keep going. Keep striving. Keep dreaming. Because the life you've always wanted is just around the corner, waiting for you to claim it. And with God on your side, there is nothing that can stop you. You are capable, you are worthy, and you have the power to create the life you've always dreamed of. So, don't ever stop believing in yourself—because you are more than enough, and your dreams are within reach. Keep moving forward. The best is yet to come.

MIND AND BODY

Before you do something that cannot be undone, think of the people who care about you, whether it's your immediate family or friends, someone who loves you despite how you feel, that darkness and that lowest point of your life, someone who still cares about you. Just imagine if other people can help others they didn't know about. How much more can you expect from those close to you? Even if you think the people you trust will lend a helping hand, they might turn their backs instead. This often reveals their true character and highlights who your real family and friends are. The problems we face daily are meant to challenge us; they form a puzzle that requires us to find the pieces to see the whole picture. It's not always easy, but the solutions are there. Remember, God has given us the tools we need: legs to take us places, arms to hold on to things, and a mind to navigate our challenges. It's no coincidence that we perceive and feel certain things; everything happens for a reason. We must approach life positively, recognizing that not everything is simply good or bad. We have to find balance in our own lives so that we may help others. We are stronger than we thought; some people never realize that because they gave up so quickly, they have a stronger mind and body than you could ever imagine.

The problems we face every day, whether big or small, are not merely obstacles to be overcome. They are challenges designed to teach us something important. Life's struggles are like a puzzle, and each piece represents a different experience or lesson. It's up to us to find those pieces and put them together to make sense of the whole picture. At first glance, the pieces might seem scattered and confusing, but in time, as we gather the experiences, the wisdom, and the insights, the full picture begins to emerge. It may not always be a perfect picture, and it may not always look like what we imagined, but it will be our picture— a reflection of our journey.

But just because life is challenging doesn't mean the answers are impossible to find. Solutions are often right in front of us, hidden in plain sight. Sometimes it just takes a shift in perspective or a change in approach to see them. We don't need to have everything figured out immediately. Life is a process, and sometimes we must learn to be patient with ourselves as we navigate through the complexities and uncertainties. Trust that the answers will come, and remember that you have everything you need to find them.

The most important tools we have at our disposal are the ones that God has already given us: our legs to take us places, our arms to hold on to what matters, and our minds to guide us through every challenge. These are the tools that allow us to move forward, to reach for new heights, to embrace change, and to grow. The mere fact that we can walk, hold, think, and dream is a gift—one that we often take for granted. We must learn to appreciate these gifts and use them to their fullest potential. Each of us is equipped with the means to rise above our circumstances, but sometimes we forget how powerful we truly are.

It's no accident that we experience the things we do in life. It might seem like events happen randomly or without reason, but there is a greater design at work. Every experience, every joy and every struggle, serves to shape us into who we are meant to become. The challenges we face are part of the process of refining our character. The people we meet, the obstacles we overcome, the lessons we learn—these are all pieces of a larger puzzle that is our life. And though we might not understand the bigger picture now, trust that everything happens for a reason. The things we go through are not meaningless; they serve to teach us, to strengthen us, and to prepare us for something greater.

As we move through life, we must learn to approach it with a sense of positivity, even when things aren't perfect. Life is rarely black and white, and there is a balance to be found in everything. Not every situation is entirely good or entirely bad. Often, things are a mix of both, and it's in finding the balance that we grow. The key is to see the beauty in both the good and the bad. Sometimes, our greatest growth comes from the most challenging moments. The pain, the loss, the disappointment—these experiences have a way of teaching us resilience, compassion, and wisdom. And while we may not always see the lesson in the moment, it will reveal itself in time.

It's easy to think that we are weaker than we are, especially when we face difficult situations. We often doubt our strength, questioning whether we can endure what life throws our way. But what I've learned is that we are much stronger than we give ourselves credit for. Many people give up too quickly, convinced that they cannot go on. They don't realize that they possess an inner strength that, once tapped into, can help them push through even the most difficult circumstances. The mind and body are more resilient than we think. We are capable of enduring much more than we realize. It's not about never feeling weak or discouraged—it's about learning to keep going even when we do. It's about finding the strength within ourselves to face whatever comes next, knowing that we are capable of handling it.

We are all capable of more than we think. Sometimes, the only thing standing between us and our potential is the belief that we can't do it. The stories we tell ourselves, the doubts we carry, and the fear of failure all work together to limit what we think we can achieve. But once we let go of those limiting beliefs and trust in our ability to face challenges, we open ourselves up to limitless possibilities. We are capable of achieving greatness, not because we are perfect, but because we are willing to try, to learn, and to keep moving forward despite the obstacles.

In this journey of life, it's important to remember that we are not alone. Even in the darkest moments, there are people who care about us, who want to help us, and who are there to lift us up when we fall. We may not always recognize them right away, but they are there, quietly supporting us in ways we might not even realize. And just as we lean on others, we must also remember to be there for those around us. Life is about connection, about supporting each other through the highs and the lows. When we come together, we are stronger than we could ever be on our own.

As you continue on your own path, take a moment to reflect on the strength you carry within you. Trust that you have everything you need to overcome whatever lies ahead. And when life gets tough, remember to lean on those who love you and, most importantly, never forget the power of your own mind and body. You are stronger than you think, and you are capable of more than you could ever imagine.

We are born into a world filled with challenges, but it is through these challenges that we find our purpose. The obstacles in life are not meant to break us, but rather to build us up. They refine our character, shape our destiny, and forge our resilience. Each challenge we face is an opportunity to grow, to learn, and to become the person we are meant to be. We are tested not because we are weak, but because we are strong enough to handle whatever comes our way.

It is easy to focus on the difficulties and forget the blessings we have. We often get caught up in what we don't have or what we've lost, but it is important to recognize what we do have. Gratitude is a powerful tool. When we focus on the things we are grateful for, we shift our perspective and open ourselves up to more positivity. By appreciating the small things, the everyday blessings, we create an environment of abundance. It's in these moments of gratitude that we find peace and strength.

As we move forward, it's crucial to remember that we are all interconnected. The way we treat others, the kindness we extend, and the love we share have a ripple effect that can change the world. No act of kindness is ever too small. Every positive action creates a wave that spreads beyond our immediate circle. By showing compassion, we inspire others to do the same, and together, we can create a world that is built on empathy, understanding, and love.

Life may be full of uncertainties, but one thing is certain: we are stronger than we think, and we have the ability to navigate whatever comes our way. With God by our side, with faith in ourselves, and with the love and support of those around us, there is no limit to what we can accomplish. Let us embrace the challenges, let us learn from the struggles, and let us never forget the strength we carry within. The journey ahead may be difficult at times, but we are more than equipped to face it. We are resilient, we are capable, and we are not alone. Together, we can overcome anything.

DRUGS & ALCOHOL:

Drugs and alcohol, substances that many use to seek solace, relaxation, or sometimes even pleasure, have a far-reaching impact on both the body and the mind. These substances, often normalized in social settings, can have devastating consequences that many people don't fully understand until it's too late. The question is, why do so many people turn to them despite knowing the potential risks? What leads someone to continue engaging with drugs or alcohol, even when they can see their lives unraveling because of it?

What does it do to our body and mind? And why do we do it? Is it beneficial? Let's stop and pause for a minute here: does it do good or bad to our body and mental health? Most of us know the answer to this question. But to answer some of these questions, what does it do to our body and mind? The answer is not good; our body suffers when our mind deteriorates; not in control of our mind is losing our body; that is why it's essential to have total control of our mind when illegal drugs and or drinking alcohol affects our thoughts and our judgments, it's like driving a car without a steering wheel, so NO it's not good. It's awful in every sense of the word and wrong in health, like overweight, diabetes, and cholesterol, to name a few, mental health issues; once it affects our brain, all hell will go loose. Drugs and alcohol destroy lives and families, and the loss of jobs and friends. Again, just to name a few, look at the news or observe what's happening in the city. There are many homeless individuals; while not all are connected to drugs and alcohol, it's evident that these substances contribute significantly to the issue. Addiction is a disease, but like any other challenge, it is possible to overcome this habit. There is a lot of help out there. That is why it's a habit you've learned throughout the years, and you can kick it little by little, one day at a time. We know it's not easy and will take time, but you must try to live your life to the fullest. Whatever reasons you are doing drugs or alcohol, that is all in the past now, and it's not coming back; reclaim your life one day at a time.

The effects of addiction can be seen all around us. In every city, there are people suffering from the consequences of substance abuse. While not all homeless individuals are struggling with addiction, it's clear that drugs and alcohol play a major role in many of these situations. They fuel the cycle of poverty, homelessness, and mental illness, trapping people in a vicious downward spiral that seems impossible to escape. Addiction is, in many ways, a disease—a chronic condition that affects the brain's reward system and alters behavior. But like any disease, it is treatable. It may take time, effort, and persistence, but recovery is possible.

Addiction is not something that happens overnight; it's a habit that often develops over time, sometimes starting with social use or experimentation and slowly growing into a dependence. But just because a habit has been ingrained in your life doesn't mean it's permanent. Recovery is possible. It might be a long road, but with determination, support, and the right mindset, it can be done. The journey may be filled with setbacks, but each day is an opportunity to make progress, to take one step forward, and to get closer to the life you truly deserve.

For those struggling with drugs or alcohol, it's essential to recognize that the past is behind you. Whatever led you to use these substances, whether it was pain, peer pressure, or something else, that is all in the past now. It's time to reclaim your life and take back control. While the path to recovery is not easy, it is one that can be walked with the right support system, the right mindset, and the belief that change is possible. One day at a time—small steps can lead to big transformations.

Remember, the journey may not be quick, and there will be challenges along the way. But there is help available, and there is always hope. Whether through therapy, support groups, or other forms of treatment, you don't have to face this challenge alone. You are not defined by your past or by the choices you've made. You have the power to change, to heal, and to create a new future for yourself. It's time to break free from the grip of addiction and live your life to the fullest, free from the chains of drugs and alcohol. It may take time, but each day you choose recovery, you are moving closer to a healthier, happier version of yourself.

Let's not forget that we all have the strength within us to make the changes we need. It may seem impossible at times, but the power to overcome addiction lies within you. With each step you take toward recovery, you are reclaiming your life. You are not alone in this journey, and there are countless resources and people who are ready to support you. Let today be the start of something new, the beginning of your path to healing, and the first day of a life that you can be proud of. One day at a time, you can overcome anything.

From the moment drugs or alcohol enter our bodies, they start to affect us in various ways. On a physical level, alcohol can impair our motor skills, slow our reflexes, and damage vital organs such as the liver, heart, and kidneys. Chronic alcohol abuse can lead to liver cirrhosis, heart disease, and digestive problems. Similarly, drugs such as cocaine, heroin, and methamphetamine can damage the brain's reward system, impair cognition, and disrupt normal brain function. These substances also take a toll on the respiratory system, cardiovascular system, and other vital organs.

The immediate effects may seem enjoyable—an altered state of consciousness, a sense of euphoria, or a temporary escape from stress. However, the long-term effects are often devastating. For instance, alcohol may give you a sense of relaxation or happiness, but over time, the body builds a tolerance, requiring more to achieve the same effects. This creates a cycle where consumption increases, and the risk of addiction heightens. Drugs, too, create similar cycles, leading users to chase the high they experienced during their first use, which only leads to deeper dependency.

The physical toll addiction takes on the body is evident in those who struggle with substance abuse. Many people develop chronic illnesses, such as respiratory issues, liver damage, and even cancer, because of their prolonged use of drugs or alcohol. These substances weaken the immune system, making it harder for the body to fight off infections and illnesses. Over time, the body becomes worn down and weakened, and the once youthful and energetic person becomes a shadow of their former self.

The Mental and Emotional Consequences

While the physical damage is clear, the mental and emotional impact of drug and alcohol abuse can be even more profound. The brain, when repeatedly exposed to these substances, starts to change. The neurochemistry of the brain becomes altered, affecting how we process emotions, think, and make decisions. The pleasure centers of the brain become hijacked, and it becomes harder for users to feel pleasure from everyday activities.

Cognitive function declines, leading to poor judgment, memory problems, and an inability to concentrate. The emotional toll is equally severe. People who struggle with addiction often find themselves trapped in a cycle of guilt, shame, and hopelessness. They feel as though they are no longer in control of their actions, and their self-esteem plummets as a result. This emotional degradation can lead to depression, anxiety, and other mental health disorders. Substance abuse becomes a way of coping with these emotions, but it is a temporary fix that only exacerbates the problem in the long run.

The impact of addiction on relationships cannot be overstated. Families are torn apart as loved ones struggle to deal with the behavior of someone who is addicted. Friends may distance themselves, unable to cope with the lies, secrecy, and manipulation that often accompany substance abuse. Relationships suffer as trust is eroded, and emotional and financial strain takes a toll. For many, addiction becomes a wall between them and those who care about them, leading to feelings of isolation and abandonment.

Breaking the Cycle

The road to recovery is never easy. For those who have been addicted to drugs or alcohol for years, the process of breaking free from these substances can feel overwhelming. The desire to change is often met with resistance, as addiction rewires the brain to make the user crave the substances even more. It takes immense strength and perseverance to overcome the hold that drugs and alcohol have on an individual, but it is possible.

The first step in recovery is acknowledging the problem. Denial is one of the biggest obstacles to healing, as many people don't want to admit that they are struggling with addiction. Recognizing that you need help is an important and courageous first step. It is crucial to understand that seeking help is not a sign of weakness, but rather a sign of strength. Reaching out to a counselor, a support group, or a trusted family member can be the first step toward recovery.

Recovery is a process, not an event. It requires patience, commitment, and resilience. The journey will be filled with ups and downs, and setbacks may occur. However, each day is an opportunity to get one step closer to living a healthy, fulfilling life. Support systems, whether through therapy, rehabilitation centers, or group meetings, can provide the necessary tools for recovery. Surrounding yourself with people who understand the struggles of addiction and who are committed to your well-being is vital.

Creating a New Life Beyond Addiction

Once a person has made the decision to turn their life around, it's important to focus on creating a new future. Recovery isn't just about abstaining from drugs or alcohol—it's about building a new, healthier lifestyle. This involves setting goals, discovering new passions, and learning how to live without the crutch of substances. Many people in recovery find joy in pursuing hobbies, focusing on their career, or spending time with loved ones in a way that fosters connection and support.

It is also essential to learn how to cope with challenges and stress without relying on substances. Life will always have its ups and downs, and it's important to build resilience to face these challenges head-on. Recovery teaches individuals to find strength in themselves and to create a life that is not defined by their addiction.

In the end, the process of overcoming addiction is about rediscovering who you are without the weight of substances controlling your life. It's about realizing your potential and embracing the future with hope and determination. While the journey may be difficult, it is a journey worth taking. Recovery is not just about surviving—it's about thriving and living a life that is fulfilling, meaningful, and free from the chains of addiction.

The Power of Hope

At the heart of recovery is hope. No matter how far gone you may feel, no matter how deep into addiction you may have sunk, there is always hope for change. You are not defined by your past mistakes or your struggles. Each new day presents an opportunity for a fresh start, and with the right support and mindset, you can turn your life around.

Remember, you are not alone. Thousands of people have walked the same path, overcome the same struggles, and emerged stronger on the other side. Recovery is not easy, but it is possible. With faith, hope, and the willingness to change, you can reclaim your life and build a future full of promise. Your story is not over—it's just beginning. Every step you take toward healing is a step closer to living the life you deserve. So, take that first step today, and never look back.

If I were an alcoholic or using illegal drugs, I would keep on reading this book until the messages get into my thick head. Because that is how I was when I was doing alcohol, I kept on listening to the audiobook "The Power of Positive Thinking" for four or five years straight every day, and finally, I got the message to help me become a better me.

SECOND CHANCE:

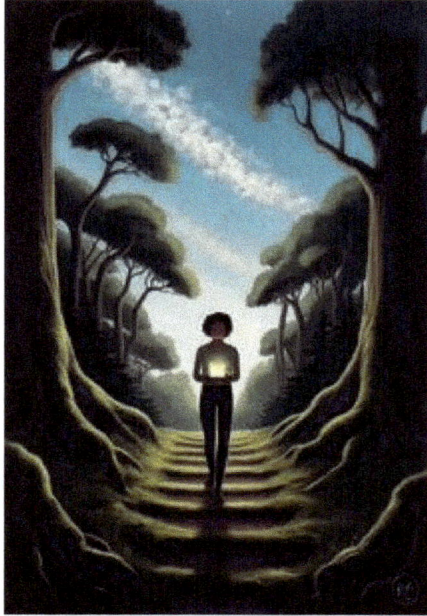

Have you in the past had a near-death experience? What would you do, or what would you change in your life? Now that you have been given a second chance in life? I never really thought about this question, and I have had many near-death experiences. It never really occurred to me that it was a nudge from above, telling me to "Hey! Wake Up!" time to change your way. All this time, I thought I was just being lucky, blessed, or not my time yet. I have been given so many chances in this life that now I realize it must have meant something. I have to change that from my old self to my new self. And I have changed my eating habits, my drinking habits, my negative thinking to positive thoughts. I also found myself praying more in my relationship with my family. Now, I pray every day, thankful for everything that I have and for more blessings that I will have. And I guess you could say that one of the reasons I wrote this book is to share with everyone that if you are reading this book, then there is still a chance for you to change, and change for the better, help your health and mental wellness to be better so that you may pass along your knowledge and blessing to other.

Your reflection on near-death experiences and the profound changes they inspired is deeply moving. It's a reminder of how fragile life is and how such moments can act as a wake-up call, urging us to reassess our priorities and embrace transformation. Near-death experiences are powerful because they strip away the distractions of daily life, leaving us face-to-face with what truly matters.

Many people go through life without taking the time to reflect on their habits, relationships, and goals until something dramatic happens. Near-death experiences have a way of shining a spotlight on the parts of ourselves that need attention. For you, the realization that these moments were more than just luck or coincidence—perhaps even divine interventions—seems to have been a turning point.

Your choice to change your eating and drinking habits, shift from negativity to positivity, and strengthen your relationship with prayer and family reflects a conscious decision to honor the second chances you've been given. These changes are not just about prolonging life but about enriching it. When we choose health, gratitude, and connection, we're investing in a future where we can give more of ourselves to the people and causes that matter most to us.

Writing a book to share this journey is a beautiful act of service. It's not just about sharing your story but about inspiring others to take charge of their own lives. Your message—that it's never too late to change—is both empowering and timely. Life is full of second chances, but recognizing them and acting on them requires courage and awareness, something you've demonstrated through your own transformation.

By encouraging readers to embrace better health and mental wellness, you're planting seeds of hope and resilience. Personal stories like yours remind others that change is possible, no matter where they are in life. Passing on blessings and knowledge, as you put it, creates a ripple effect, where your experiences can positively influence countless others.

It's worth reflecting on how these near-death experiences have not only changed your perspective but also deepened your sense of purpose. You're living proof that adversity can lead to growth, and that even the darkest moments can illuminate a path to a brighter, more meaningful future. Your journey of gratitude, faith, and transformation is an inspiring testament to the power of resilience and the enduring potential for positive change.

Near-death experiences have a way of stripping away the unimportant and leaving us face-to-face with what truly matters. It's as if life presses pause for a brief, terrifying moment, forcing us to look at ourselves, our choices, and the direction we're heading. For some, these moments are fleeting, forgotten as life resumes its hectic pace. For others, like myself, they become pivotal points, reminders that life is fragile and that every day is a gift.

I've had several near-death experiences in my life. At first, I brushed them off as sheer luck or coincidence. I thought, *well, that was close. Guess I dodged a bullet there.* But as the close calls added up, I began to question whether these moments were random or if there was a deeper meaning. Was life trying to tell me something? Was there a purpose behind these narrow escapes? I started to feel that these experiences were not mere accidents but divine interventions—a nudge from above, saying, *Hey! Wake up! It's time to change.*

The realization hit me like a lightning bolt: these weren't just moments of survival. They were opportunities, second chances, gifts that I hadn't earned but had been given nonetheless. I could no longer live as I had before, taking these chances for granted. I knew it was time to reflect deeply and make meaningful changes in my life.

A Journey of Transformation

My journey of transformation began with small steps. The first thing I realized was that I needed to take better care of my physical health. I had always lived as though my body was invincible, indulging in unhealthy eating and drinking habits, ignoring the warning signs that my lifestyle was taking a toll. But those near-death moments reminded me that my body is not just a vessel; it's a gift that I need to nurture and protect.

I started by changing my eating habits. It wasn't easy at first—I had to unlearn years of bad habits and develop new ones. I began incorporating more fruits, vegetables, and whole foods into my diet, reducing processed and sugary foods. I learned to cook meals that nourished my body rather than just filling my stomach. Slowly but surely, I felt the difference. My energy levels improved, and I felt more vibrant and alive.

Drinking was another area where I had to make significant changes. It wasn't just about cutting back on alcohol; it was about understanding why I was drinking in the first place. Was I using it as a coping mechanism? Was it a social habit I had never questioned? Once I addressed the root causes, it became easier to make healthier choices.

As my physical health improved, I noticed another shift: my thoughts became clearer, and my mindset began to change. I realized how much of my mental energy had been consumed by negativity—worrying about the past, fearing the future, and dwelling on things I couldn't control. It was as if those near-death experiences had jolted me into a new awareness, reminding me that life is too short to waste on negativity.

I began to practice gratitude intentionally. Every day, I took a few moments to reflect on the things I was thankful for—my family, my health, the beauty of nature, the kindness of strangers. This simple practice had a profound impact on my mental wellness. It shifted my focus from what was lacking in my life to what was abundant.

Strengthening Relationships

Another significant change was in my relationships. Near-death experiences have a way of making you reevaluate who and what matters most in your life. For me, it was my family. I realized that I had taken them for granted far too often, assuming they would always be there. But those close calls reminded me how fleeting life can be and how precious the time we have with our loved ones is.

I made a conscious effort to strengthen my relationships, starting with small gestures: a phone call to check in, a handwritten note to express my love, a hug that lingered a little longer. I also worked on being more present when I was with them, putting away distractions and truly listening. These efforts brought us closer together and created memories I'll cherish forever.

A Newfound Faith

Perhaps one of the most profound changes was in my spiritual life. Before, I had a passive relationship with faith—it was there, but it wasn't central to my life. The near-death experiences changed that. They made me realize how much I had to be thankful for and how much I needed to rely on a higher power.

I started praying more—not just in moments of need but as a daily practice. Prayer became a way for me to express gratitude, seek guidance, and find peace. It deepened my sense of purpose and gave me the strength to face challenges with a calm and steady heart. My faith became a source of comfort and a wellspring of hope, grounding me in times of uncertainty.

Sharing the Journey

One of the reasons I decided to write this book is because I wanted to share my journey with others. I wanted to show that it's never too late to change, no matter how many mistakes you've made or how stuck you feel. If you're reading this, then you've been given the same gift I was: the chance to change, to start fresh, to create a life that reflects your values and aspirations.

Change isn't easy, but it's worth it. It starts with small steps—a healthier meal, a kind word, a moment of gratitude—but those small steps add up. Over time, they transform not just your habits but your entire outlook on life.

I believe that when we make positive changes in our own lives, we create a ripple effect that extends to those around us. By improving our health and mental wellness, we're better equipped to support and inspire others. By sharing our stories, we remind people that they're not alone and that change is possible.

Lessons from Near-Death Experiences

Looking back, I realize that each near-death experience taught me something valuable. They were lessons disguised as close calls, reminders to live with intention and purpose. Here are some of the lessons I've learned:

1. **Life is fragile.** Every moment is a gift, and we shouldn't take it for granted.

2. **Health is wealth.** Taking care of our bodies is one of the most important investments we can make.

3. **Gratitude is powerful.** Focusing on what we have rather than what we lack can transform our perspective.

4. **Relationships matter.** The people in our lives are our greatest treasures, and we should nurture those connections.

5. **Faith is a foundation.** Whether it's faith in a higher power, in ourselves, or in the goodness of others, faith gives us strength and hope.

As I continue this journey, I know there will be challenges ahead. Life is unpredictable, and no one is immune to setbacks. But I've learned that it's not about avoiding challenges—it's about facing them with courage and resilience.

Each day is an opportunity to grow, to learn, and to become a better version of ourselves. I've made it my mission to live with intention, to embrace change, and to use my experiences to inspire others. If my story can help even one person take that first step toward a healthier, happier life, then it's all been worth it.

To anyone reading this: know that it's never too late to change. Whether you've faced near-death experiences or are simply searching for a new direction, you have the power to transform your life. Start small, stay committed, and remember that every step forward is a victory. Life is a journey, and it's up to us to make it a meaningful one.

The Fragility of Life

There's something humbling about coming face-to-face with your own mortality. It strips away the illusions we build around ourselves— illusions of invincibility, permanence, and endless time. In those moments when life hangs by a thread, you see with startling clarity just how fragile it all is. The simple act of breathing, which we so often take for granted, becomes a gift. The heartbeat, a rhythm so constant we barely notice it, becomes a song of life.

I've had several moments where that rhythm was nearly silenced, where the gift of breath was almost taken away. Looking back, I realize how those experiences shaped me, even when I didn't recognize it at the time. They were like punctuation marks in the story of my life, forcing me to pause and consider the path I was on.

Revisiting Those Moments

One particular near-death experience stands out vividly in my memory. I was in a car accident that could have easily ended my life. The sound of screeching tires, the crunch of metal, and the sudden, jarring stillness that followed—it all happened in a matter of seconds, but those seconds felt like an eternity.

In the aftermath, as I sat trembling and in shock, I remember thinking *that could have been it. That could have been the end of my story.* It wasn't just the physical impact that shook me; it was the realization of how much I had left undone. There were dreams I hadn't pursued, words I hadn't said, and relationships I hadn't nurtured.

Another time, I experienced a severe health scare. For days, I was bedridden, unsure of what the outcome would be. It was during those long hours of solitude that I confronted some hard truths about the way I had been living. I had been neglecting my health, pushing my body to its limits without giving it the care it deserved. I had been so focused on the external—career, responsibilities, obligations—that I had forgotten to tend to the internal.

These moments, as terrifying as they were, became catalysts for change. They were like mirrors, reflecting back to me the areas of my life that needed attention, healing, and transformation.

The Power of Second Chances

When you survive a near-death experience, it's impossible not to see life differently. Each new day feels like a bonus round, a precious opportunity to rewrite your story. It's as though the universe is saying, *here's another chance—what will you do with it?*

For me, those second chances became a call to action. I knew I couldn't go back to living the way I had been. Something had to change, and it had to change now.

The first step was to embrace gratitude. It sounds simple, but gratitude has a way of transforming your perspective. Instead of focusing on what's lacking or what's wrong, you begin to see all the blessings you've been given. Even on the hardest days, there's always something to be thankful for—a kind word, a warm meal, a moment of peace.

I started keeping a gratitude journal, jotting down three things I was thankful for each day. At first, it felt awkward, almost forced. But over time, it became a habit, and that habit became a mindset. Gratitude shifted the way I saw the world, allowing me to find joy in the little things and resilience in the face of challenges.

Building a Healthier Life

Another major area of focus was my health. I realized that if I wanted to make the most of this second chance, I needed to take better care of my body. It wasn't about vanity or perfection—it was about respecting the vessel that carries me through life.

I began by making small, manageable changes. I swapped processed foods for whole, nutrient-rich options. I incorporated more fruits and vegetables into my meals, drank more water, and paid attention to portion sizes. Exercise became a regular part of my routine, not as a chore but as a form of self-care.

Over time, these changes added up. I felt stronger, more energetic, and more in tune with my body. But perhaps even more importantly, I felt a sense of pride and empowerment. Taking care of my health wasn't just about physical well-being; it was an act of self-love and a way of honoring the second chance I had been given.

Redefining Success

One of the most profound lessons I learned was the need to redefine success. Before my near-death experiences, I had fallen into the trap of equating success with external achievements—career milestones, financial stability, social recognition. But in those moments when my life was on the line, none of those things mattered. What mattered were the people I loved, the memories I had created, and the legacy I would leave behind.

Success, I realized, isn't about accumulating wealth or accolades; it's about living a life of purpose, authenticity, and connection. It's about being true to yourself and making a positive impact on the world around you.

This shift in perspective freed me from the pressure of always striving for more. Instead of chasing external validation, I began to focus on what truly brought me joy and fulfillment. I pursued hobbies that made me happy, spent more time with loved ones, and looked for ways to contribute to my community.

Strengthening Faith

Another transformative aspect of my journey was the deepening of my faith. Those near-death experiences reminded me of the presence of something greater than myself—whether you call it God, the universe, or a higher power. I felt a sense of divine guidance, a reassurance that I was being watched over and protected.

This renewed faith became a source of strength and comfort. I began to pray more, not just in moments of need but as a daily practice. Prayer became a way to express gratitude, seek guidance, and find peace. It also helped me let go of the things I couldn't control, trusting that everything happens for a reason and that I was exactly where I was meant to be.

Sharing the Message

One of the reasons I felt compelled to write this book was to share these lessons with others. If my experiences can inspire even one person to make a positive change, to embrace gratitude, or to live with greater intention, then it will all have been worth it.

Life is unpredictable, and none of us knows how much time we have. But what we do know is that each moment is an opportunity to grow, to connect, and to make a difference. If you've been given a second chance—whether through a near-death experience or simply through the gift of waking up each morning—don't waste it. Use it to become the best version of yourself and to create a life that you're proud of.

The journey of transformation is ongoing. I still have moments of doubt, fear, and struggle, but I face them with a renewed sense of purpose and resilience. I know that life isn't about being perfect; it's about showing up, trying your best, and learning from every experience.

If there's one thing I hope you take away from my story, it's this: You have the power to change your life. Whether you're facing a health challenge, a personal setback, or simply the realization that you're not living the life you want, you can start fresh. You can make choices that align with your values, nurture your well-being, and bring you closer to your goals.

Don't wait for a near-death experience to wake you up. Let this be your reminder to live fully, love deeply, and embrace each day with gratitude. Lives is a gift—cherish it, celebrate it, and use it to make a difference.

MEMORIES

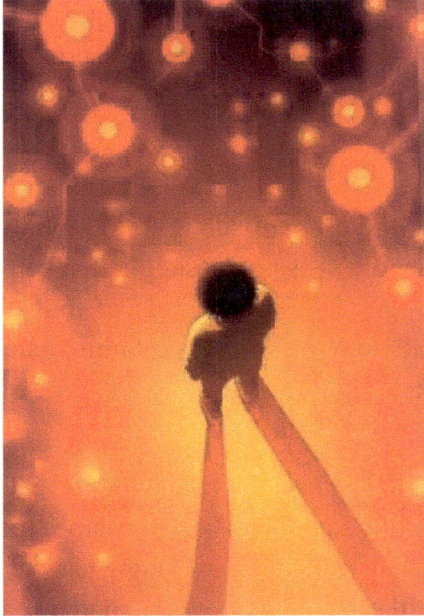

THE MORE YOU THINK ABOUT THE BAD TIME, the more you miss the good time. Yes, memories can be good and evil. It's an experience that we had in the past, and it's nice to reminisce, especially the good ones that we often put in pictures and sometimes in videos so that we may revisit it and enlighten ourselves. Remember the good old days and the happy times with family or friends, but let's not forget the memories of bad times, the hard times, and the challenging events we had. It's unfortunate, but these memories are the ones that develop who we are; the painful memories and the mistakes are the ones that make us. It teaches us to grow and be better. We learned from those, and now you can handle the situation better. Memories, good or bad, are in the past; we may cherish them, laugh about them, cry about them, or learn about them, but we must move on and try to be better from those experiences.

Memories are the treasures of our minds, locked away in the vault of our consciousness, waiting to be revisited. They are a collection of moments that shape who we are—some are golden, sparkling with joy, and others are dark, etched with pain. Yet, it is this duality that gives memories their power. They remind us of where we've been and teach us how to navigate where we are going.

The Power of Good Memories

Good memories are like warm sunlight on a chilly day. They bring comfort, warmth, and a sense of nostalgia that can brighten even the gloomiest of moments. They remind us of the times when life felt simple, joyous, and carefree. Birthdays, family gatherings, first loves, childhood adventures—these moments are etched into our hearts, becoming a part of who we are.

Looking at old photographs or replaying a cherished video can transport us back in time, filling us with the same emotions we felt then. These memories are like anchors, grounding us when life feels chaotic. They remind us of the happiness we've experienced and give us hope that such moments can happen again.

However, while good memories are a source of joy, they can also be bittersweet. They remind us of what once was but can never be exactly the same again. Loved ones we've lost, places we can no longer visit, or phases of life we've outgrown—they all become a part of our cherished past, a beautiful reminder to appreciate the present moment.

The Lessons in Painful Memories

On the other side of the coin are the painful memories—the moments of heartbreak, failure, and loss. These are the memories we often wish we could forget, yet they are the ones that shape us the most. It's through these difficult experiences that we grow, learn, and develop resilience.

Painful memories are teachers, albeit harsh ones. They show us our limits and, more importantly, how to surpass them. They teach us the importance of perseverance, empathy, and forgiveness. A failed relationship may teach us about self-worth and boundaries. A career setback might push us to discover our true passion. The loss of a loved one teaches us to cherish the people we have while they're still here.

It's natural to want to avoid or suppress painful memories, but doing so robs us of the lessons they hold. Instead, by confronting them and reflecting on them, we can find meaning in the pain and use it as fuel for personal growth.

The Balance Between Reminiscing and Moving Forward

While memories are invaluable, it's important not to dwell on them too much, especially the painful ones. The more we replay the bad times in our minds, the more we miss out on the good times happening right now. Life is a journey forward, and while our memories are part of our story, they are not the whole story.

Cherishing good memories is a wonderful thing, but it's essential not to live in the past. Sometimes, we get so caught up in "the good old days" that we forget to create new memories. Similarly, replaying painful memories repeatedly can trap us in a cycle of regret or resentment.

The key is to strike a balance:

- **Reflect but don't dwell.** Look back to learn or find joy, but always return to the present moment.

- **Honor your past but focus on your future.** Use your memories as stepping stones to build a better life.

- **Appreciate the now.** Each day offers opportunities to create new, meaningful memories.

Memories as Motivation

Both good and bad memories can serve as powerful motivators. Good memories remind us of what's possible and inspire us to seek more joy, love, and connection. Bad memories, on the other hand, show us what we've overcome and prove that we're capable of handling life's challenges.

For instance, think about a time when you faced a significant struggle. Maybe it was a tough exam, a financial hardship, or a difficult relationship. At the time, it might have felt insurmountable. But now, looking back, you realize how much strength and determination you had. That memory becomes a source of confidence, reminding you that you can face future challenges with the same courage.

Good memories, meanwhile, can motivate us to recreate those joyful moments. If you have fond memories of family vacations, you might be inspired to plan more trips with your loved ones. If you remember the pride of achieving a goal, you might be motivated to set new ones and work toward them.

The Role of Memories in Relationships

Memories play a significant role in our relationships with others. They are the glue that binds us to the people we love. Shared experiences, inside jokes, and heartfelt moments create a tapestry of connection that strengthens our bonds.

At the same time, memories can also create rifts if they're associated with unresolved conflicts or misunderstandings. It's crucial to address these painful memories within relationships, seeking forgiveness and understanding where possible. Healing these wounds can pave the way for healthier, more fulfilling connections.

Turning Memories Into Action

Rather than just reminiscing about memories, we can use them as a guide for how we want to live. Here are a few ways to do that:

1. **Celebrate the Good.** Look back on your happiest memories and think about what made them so special. Was it the people,

the activities, or the mindset you had? Use this insight to bring more of those elements into your life now.

2. **Learn from the Bad.** Reflect on painful memories with a sense of curiosity rather than judgment. What lessons can you take from those experiences? How can you apply those lessons to your current life?

3. **Create New Memories.** Don't let your past define you. Actively seek out opportunities to create new, meaningful experiences. Spend time with loved ones, pursue your passions, and step out of your comfort zone.

4. **Share Your Stories.** Memories are meant to be shared. By telling your stories, you not only preserve them but also inspire and connect with others.

Memories as a Source of Gratitude

Ultimately, memories—both good and bad—are a testament to the fact that we've lived, loved, and experienced the richness of life. They remind us of all the moments, big and small, that have brought us to where we are today.

Gratitude is the thread that ties it all together. When we look back with gratitude, we find value in even the most difficult experiences. We see the beauty in our struggles and the blessings in our joys.

So, as you reflect on your memories, let them be a source of inspiration. Cherish the good times, learn from the bad, and use them all to guide you as you move forward. Life is a continuous journey of creating, remembering, and growing—and every memory is a chapter in the story of who you are.

FEAR:

So, when the fear kicks in, it's just a way of our body protecting ourselves; it's a defense mechanism, and everybody has one. It's essential to our feelings or senses; we can't always be brave. Otherwise, we can get into trouble or hurt ourselves. Fear makes you think twice; it gives you that pause before you react to something. Sometimes, that something can be scary, but it is still an emotion or feeling. I am no psychologist, but this is just my opinion; I believe that there are two kinds of fear, first is the instantaneous one, the one that happens all of a sudden, and then there is the fear we installed in our mind, the one that hasn't happened yet. Still, we are so afraid of the result or the outcome of things that we don't even know what they are. It's a fear of losing or winning, a fear of the results that it's going to be good or it's going to be wrong; this kind of fear is often the result of us not succeeding in life because of the thought of "what if." We should think, "If I don't do this now," or "This time is better than any other time."

We should be thinking more positively, whatever the outcome may be. I like this quote: "It's not the journey; it's the Destination." There will always be challenges; we must conquer that fear to pass this challenging life.

Fear is one of the most primal and universal emotions that every human experiences. It transcends cultures, ages, and circumstances, binding us together in our shared vulnerability. At its core, fear is not inherently bad—it's a natural defense mechanism designed to protect us. When fear kicks in, it's our body's way of saying, *"Pay attention; something needs your focus."* It's a signal, a survival instinct deeply embedded in our biology. Yet, fear can be a double-edged sword. While it can shield us from harm, it can also become a barrier that holds us back from living fully and embracing life's opportunities.

The Dual Nature of Fear

As you've aptly pointed out, fear manifests in two primary forms: **instantaneous fear** and **anticipatory fear.** Each serves a different purpose, and understanding these distinctions can empower us to respond rather than react.

1. **Instantaneous Fear:**

   This type of fear arises in the moment. It's that adrenaline-fueled rush you feel when a car swerves unexpectedly into your lane or when you hear a loud noise in the dark. This kind of fear is deeply tied to our survival instincts, triggering the *fight, flight, or freeze* response. It sharpens our senses, quickens our reflexes, and prepares our body to handle immediate threats. While it might feel overwhelming, this fear is often short-lived and dissipates once the danger is gone. It's a protector—a guardian urging us to stay safe.

2. **Anticipatory Fear:**

   Unlike its instantaneous counterpart, anticipatory fear isn't based on what's happening right now but on what *might* happen. It's the fear of the unknown, the "what ifs" that swirl in our minds. Will I fail this test? What if I embarrass myself in front of others? What if this decision leads to disaster? This fear is more insidious because it stems from uncertainty and often has no tangible threat. It exists entirely in our minds, feeding on doubt, insecurity, and past failures. While it may feel less urgent than immediate fear, anticipatory fear can be more debilitating, as it stops us from pursuing our dreams or taking necessary risks.

Fear as a Tool for Growth

Although fear can feel overwhelming, it doesn't have to be our enemy. In fact, fear can be a powerful teacher and motivator if we learn to approach it with the right mindset. Recognizing fear as an emotion— one that is temporary and not all-consuming—can help us put it in perspective.

- **Fear Offers Pause:**

  Instantaneous fear forces us to pause and evaluate a situation. This pause is essential; it prevents impulsive actions that might lead to harm. For example, fear might stop you from stepping into a busy street without looking both ways. In this way, fear is not a weakness but a strength—it's your body and mind working together to ensure your well-being.

- **Fear Challenges Comfort Zones:**

  Anticipatory fear often arises when we're on the cusp of growth. It signals that we're stepping into unfamiliar territory, trying something new, or striving for a goal that feels just out of reach. While this fear can be paralyzing, it also holds the key to personal development. Facing it head-on allows us to expand our horizons, build resilience, and achieve things we once thought impossible.

The Trap of "What If"

One of the greatest challenges with anticipatory fear is its tendency to trap us in a cycle of *what ifs*. This fear often whispers, *"What if I fail? What if I get hurt? What if this isn't the right decision?"* These thoughts can snowball, creating an overwhelming sense of dread and uncertainty.

But what if we reframed these questions? Instead of focusing on the negative possibilities, we could ask, *"What if I succeed? What if this leads to something incredible? What if this is exactly what I need to grow?"* By shifting our perspective, we take away fear's power to control us and instead use it as fuel for action.

Conquering Fear Through Action

The best way to overcome fear—particularly anticipatory fear—is through action. Fear thrives on inaction and hesitation. The longer we dwell on it, the stronger it becomes. But the moment we take a step forward, fear begins to lose its grip.

1. **Embrace the Present Moment:**

Fear often pulls us away from the present, forcing us to dwell on past mistakes or future uncertainties. Grounding ourselves in the present moment can help combat this. Techniques like mindfulness and deep breathing can anchor us, allowing us to see fear for what it is: a fleeting emotion rather than a permanent state.

2. **Break Down the Challenge:**

Large tasks or goals can feel overwhelming, feeding our anticipatory fear. By breaking them down into smaller, manageable steps, we can approach them with more confidence. Each small success builds momentum and diminishes the power of fear.

3. **Reframe Failure:**

One of the biggest sources of anticipatory fear is the fear of failure. But failure isn't the end—it's a stepping stone to success. Every great achievement is built on a foundation of setbacks and lessons learned. When we stop viewing failure as something to fear and start seeing it as an opportunity for growth, we take away its power to paralyze us.

4. **Lean on Support Systems:**

Facing fear doesn't mean doing it alone. Friends, family, mentors, and even therapists can provide encouragement, guidance, and perspective. Sharing your fears with others often makes them feel less daunting and more manageable.

The Role of Positive Thinking

As you wisely noted, a positive mindset is a powerful antidote to fear. It's easy to let fear pull us into a spiral of negativity, but choosing to focus on the potential for good can make all the difference. This doesn't mean ignoring risks or challenges—it means approaching them with hope and determination.

- **Visualize Success:**

Instead of imagining all the ways something could go wrong, visualize yourself succeeding. Picture the steps you'll take, the obstacles you'll overcome, and the joy you'll feel when you achieve your goal. This mental rehearsal can boost your confidence and reduce fear.

- **Affirm Your Strengths:**

  Remind yourself of times you've faced challenges and come out stronger. Reflecting on past successes can help you build the courage to tackle new fears.

"It's Not the Journey; It's the Destination"

This quote beautifully encapsulates the importance of pushing through fear. Life is filled with challenges, but each one brings us closer to our ultimate goals. Fear is just one part of the journey—it doesn't define the destination. By embracing fear, learning from it, and moving forward despite it, we can navigate life's challenges with courage and grace.

The Legacy of Conquering Fear

When we face our fears, we don't just overcome the immediate challenge—we set a precedent for how we'll handle challenges in the future. Each time we conquer fear, we build resilience, confidence, and a sense of empowerment. This not only benefits us but also inspires those around us. By showing others that fear is not an insurmountable obstacle, we encourage them to face their own fears and strive for their dreams.

In the end, fear is not something to be eradicated—it's something to be understood, embraced, and harnessed. It's a natural part of being human, a companion on the journey of life. When we stop running from fear and start working with it, we unlock our full potential and discover the strength that lies within us. Life will always have its challenges, but with the right mindset, we can conquer them all, one step at a time.

Fear is an emotion that is as ancient as life itself. It has evolved over millennia to serve a singular purpose: survival. From the early days of humanity, when fear drove us to flee from predators or defend against rival tribes, to the modern era, where it manifests in the form of anxieties over career, relationships, or personal growth, fear has remained a constant presence. Its function, however, is not to paralyze us but to sharpen our senses, warn us of danger, and, when understood properly, propel us toward meaningful action.

Yet fear is complex—it is both our protector and, at times, our greatest adversary. To conquer fear is not necessarily to vanquish it but to understand its nature and learn to live alongside it, channeling its energy into something constructive. To expand upon this intricate topic, let us delve into the origins of fear, its psychological implications, and the strategies to transform it into a source of strength.

When we experience fear, our body undergoes a cascade of reactions. It begins in the brain, specifically in the amygdala, a small almond-shaped structure responsible for processing emotions. Upon detecting a threat—whether physical, emotional, or imagined—the amygdala sends a distress signal to the hypothalamus. This triggers the activation of the sympathetic nervous system, commonly known as the *fight, flight, or freeze* response.

During this state:

- **The heart rate increases,** pumping more blood to muscles and vital organs.

- **Breathing quickens,** providing more oxygen to the brain and body.

- **The pupils dilate,** improving vision to better assess the surroundings.

- **Non-essential functions,** such as digestion, temporarily shut down to conserve energy for survival.

While these responses are lifesaving in moments of real danger, the brain does not always differentiate between tangible threats (a predator or physical harm) and perceived threats (fear of public speaking, rejection, or failure). As a result, the same physiological responses can occur even when the threat exists only in our minds.

While the physical manifestations of fear are rooted in biology, its psychological effects are profoundly nuanced. Fear can shape our thoughts, influence our decisions, and, if left unchecked, dominate our lives. To understand this better, let us explore the two primary dimensions of fear: **immediate fear** and **anticipatory fear.**

1. **Immediate Fear:**

   Immediate fear is visceral and reactionary. It arises in response to an external stimulus—a sudden noise in the dark, a near-miss car accident, or an aggressive confrontation. In such moments, fear serves its evolutionary purpose: it prioritizes survival above all else. While intense, this type of fear is typically short-lived and subsides once the threat has passed.

Anticipatory Fear:

Anticipatory fear, on the other hand, is rooted in the mind's ability to imagine the future. Unlike immediate fear, it is not tied to a present danger but to a potential one. It is the fear of failure, rejection, or the unknown. This type of fear often manifests as anxiety, worry, or self-doubt, and it has the power to hinder personal growth and prevent us from taking risks. To classify fear as either "good" or "bad" is to oversimplify its complexity. Fear can be both a friend and a foe, depending on how we respond to it.

- **Fear as a Friend:**

  When harnessed correctly, fear can be a powerful motivator. It pushes us to prepare, adapt, and grow. For instance, the fear of failing an exam might compel a student to study harder, while the fear of losing a loved one can deepen our appreciation for the time we have together. In these cases, fear serves as a catalyst for positive action.

- **Fear as a Foe:**

  Conversely, fear becomes detrimental when it paralyzes us. It can prevent us from taking necessary risks, pursuing opportunities, or even living fully. The fear of rejection might stop someone from expressing their feelings, while the fear of failure could deter someone from chasing their dreams. This is the kind of fear that must be confronted and overcome.

One of fear's most insidious forms is the "what if" trap—a cycle of anticipatory fear that revolves around imagined worst-case scenarios.

- *What if I fail?*
- *What if I'm not good enough?*
- *What if things don't work out?*

These questions are often born out of self-doubt and a lack of confidence. They keep us stuck in a loop of inaction, preventing us from taking steps toward our goals.

But what if we reframed these questions? Instead of asking, *"What if I fail?"* we might ask, *"What if I succeed?"* By shifting our perspective, we turn fear into a source of hope and possibility.

In today's world, fear is less about physical survival and more about navigating complex social, emotional, and professional landscapes. Fear of public speaking, fear of rejection, fear of failure—these are the modern predators that stalk us. While they may not threaten our lives, they can threaten our sense of self-worth and fulfillment.

However, it's important to remember that fear, even in these contexts, is not inherently bad. It signals areas where we need to grow. For example:

- **Fear of public speaking** might indicate a need to build confidence and communication skills.

- **Fear of failure** might point to perfectionism or unrealistic expectations.

- **Fear of rejection** could highlight insecurities or a lack of self-acceptance.

Strategies for Conquering Fear

Acknowledge the Fear:

The first step in overcoming fear is to acknowledge its presence. Denying or suppressing fear only gives it more power. By admitting that you're afraid, you take the first step toward understanding and addressing it.

Understand the Root Cause:

Ask yourself: *What am I really afraid of?* Often, the surface-level fear is masking a deeper issue. For instance, the fear of public speaking might stem from a fear of judgment or a lack of self-confidence. Understanding the root cause allows you to address the underlying issue.

Take Incremental Steps:

Facing fear doesn't mean diving into the deep end all at once. Start small. If you're afraid of public speaking, practice in front of a trusted friend before speaking to a larger audience. Gradual exposure builds confidence and reduces fear over time.

Reframe Negative Thoughts: Replace negative "what if" scenarios with positive ones. Instead of focusing on what could go wrong, imagine what could go right. Visualize yourself succeeding and thriving in the face of fear.

Focus on the Present: Fear often pulls us into the future, filling our minds with worries about what might happen. Grounding yourself in the present moment through mindfulness or meditation can help quiet these anxieties and bring clarity.

Seek Support: You don't have to face fear alone. Friends, family, mentors, or therapists can provide guidance, encouragement, and perspective. Sometimes, just talking about your fears can make them feel more manageable.

Ultimately, fear is one of life's greatest teachers. It challenges us, pushes us to grow, and reveals our inner strength. By embracing fear—rather than running from it—we unlock new possibilities and discover what we are truly capable of. As the quote goes, *"Feel the fear and do it anyway."* Fear may never disappear entirely, but by learning to coexist with it, we can live fuller, more meaningful lives. Whether it's the fear of failure, rejection, or the unknown, every fear we face is an opportunity to grow. So the next time fear whispers in your ear, don't let it stop you. Instead, let it guide you toward your next adventure.

DEATH

Death is a concept that shadows every human life. Its inevitability gives it power, and its mystery evokes fear, curiosity, and contemplation. For some, it is a distant reality; for others, it feels as close as the next breath. Yet, there is another kind of death—one not of the body but of the soul, hope, or spirit. To face such darkness is profoundly isolating, but it is also an opportunity for transformation.

Death may have entered my life at least a dozen times, but it never did take me away. Once, I was in the darkest moments of my life. I almost did take my life, and during my darkest hours, I've thought of driving my car at high speed and crash my car to the wall, I've thought of driving my car to the freeway and driving through the bridge, thought of jumping off the building, even thought of cutting my wrist and bleed it out. It was just a thought because something was pulling or holding me back. And it was my family; they had no idea what was going through my head, but my wife and two daughters were hovering in my head and my heart. I thought of killing myself so that they could inherit my life insurance, my social security benefits/pension, and the money that my wife and kids could get to my work. But I asked myself, would that make my wife and kids happy? Will money solve all of my troubles? If I do take my own life, who is going to protect them when I'm gone? Who will do all the man's job at our house when I'm gone? I must reflect upon my decision; after all the thinking and soul-searching, I surrender to the lord, the creator of heaven and earth and all things. I don't know your religion; only one god created heaven and earth. Surrender yourself, give it all to him, and let him guide you; if you believe your god is good, he will not lead you to the wrong path.

I know because my god is good; after I surrender everything to him, my life has improved, and my thoughts are much more straightforward. After that day, when I gave it all to him, I fear nothing; I feel no pain. I feel guided and know I'm going to a better place. I have a renewed life as if I have a second life. Considering I almost died multiple times. Turn your back from the darkness and face the light. I allowed myself to change from negative thoughts to a positive attitude. I have changed my bad habits to a good habit. The changes may be slow, but I know it's for the better. God is always good; all the time, god is good. Have faith, believe.

When death visits our thoughts, it is often accompanied by feelings of despair, worthlessness, and overwhelming burden. These moments are some of the most challenging trials a person can endure. The idea that the end could bring peace or relief from pain becomes seductive, wrapping its tendrils around the mind and suffocating hope.

I have known this darkness. At my lowest, death was not merely an abstract concept but an idea I entertained seriously. I imagined myself in scenarios where my own actions would end the unbearable weight of my existence. Driving at high speed into a wall, careening off a bridge, jumping from a great height, or even bleeding myself dry—these thoughts were not fleeting. They were vivid, persistent, and haunting.

152

But in those moments, even when death felt like a solution, a faint whisper always held me back. It wasn't a voice, nor was it logic. It was love—the thought of my family. My wife and two daughters, unaware of my internal battles, became the invisible force tethering me to this world.

One of the most devastating aspects of contemplating death is the rationalization that it could somehow benefit those we leave behind. I convinced myself that my life insurance, social security benefits, and pensions might ease the financial burdens my family faced. I thought that removing myself from their lives would be an ultimate act of selflessness.

But then I asked myself:

- *Would money fill the void of my absence?*
- *Would my wife and daughters truly be happier without me?*
- *Who would protect them, guide them, and share in their lives if I were gone?*

These questions pierced through the darkness. The answers were clear: they would suffer more from my loss than from any material hardship. My role in their lives was irreplaceable—not because I was perfect, but because I was theirs. In my search for meaning and salvation from these suffocating thoughts, I turned to my faith. I surrendered myself to the Creator—the one who made heaven and earth and all things within it. My belief may differ from yours, but the essence remains universal: I sought refuge in something greater than myself.

By surrendering my burdens to God, I found relief. It wasn't an instant transformation, nor did my problems vanish overnight. What changed was my perspective. I no longer carried the weight of my despair alone. I felt guided, as though an unseen hand was leading me away from the abyss and toward the light.

For me, God became the source of renewed strength and clarity. My faith assured me that life, no matter how heavy, was worth living. I began to see challenges not as punishments but as opportunities for growth.

Emerging from such darkness feels like being granted a second life. When I look back at those times, I realize how close I came to letting go and how much I would have missed. My life now is far from perfect, but it is filled with purpose.

- **Fear no longer rules me.** By placing my trust in God, I feel equipped to face whatever lies ahead. The unknown no longer terrifies me; it motivates me.

- **Pain is no longer my enemy.** I have learned to see pain as a teacher. It reminds me of my resilience and the value of every breath.

- **Hope is my anchor.** Even in difficult times, I hold onto the belief that things will improve.

One of the most critical steps in overcoming despair is actively choosing to turn away from negative thoughts and habits. It's not easy. The darkness often feels comforting in its familiarity, while the light demands effort, vulnerability, and faith. But the reward is immeasurable.

Adopting Positive Habits: Change begins with small steps. For me, this meant letting go of harmful behaviors and replacing them with constructive actions—whether it was focusing on my health, engaging with my family, or deepening my spiritual practices.

Embracing Slow Progress: Change is rarely immediate. It's a gradual process, filled with setbacks and small victories. Patience became my ally, reminding me that every step forward, no matter how small, was progress.

Leaning on Faith: Whenever doubt or despair crept back, I turned to prayer and reflection. My faith became a constant source of reassurance and strength.

For me, faith was the lifeline that pulled me from the depths. My God, whom I believe is always good, gave me the strength to continue. Your faith may take a different form, but the essence remains the same: placing your trust in something greater than yourself can bring peace, purpose, and healing.

Surrendering to God doesn't mean giving up control; it means accepting that you don't have to face life's challenges alone. Whether you call him God, Creator, or another name, the divine presence is a source of hope and guidance. Today, I wake up with gratitude—not because my life is free from challenges but because I have been given the strength to face them. I cherish my family, my faith, and the lessons I've learned through struggle.

Death may visit our thoughts, but it does not have to claim our spirit. There is always a path forward, even when we cannot see it. By turning away from darkness and embracing the light, we can find meaning, purpose, and peace. If you are struggling, take heart: your life is a gift, and your story is still unfolding. Turn to faith, love, and hope, and you will discover that the light is never far away.

SEVEN MORTAL SINS

The Seven Mortal Sins—pride, greed, lust, envy, gluttony, wrath, and sloth—have been long regarded as dangerous vices that lead to spiritual and moral downfall. When considering how these sins might contribute to something as grave as suicide, it becomes a sobering analysis of how deeply intertwined human behaviors and emotions can be. Each sin can represent a pathway to despair, self-destruction, or harm to others. However, understanding their connection to mental health and well-being also offers an opportunity for healing and transformation.

For some odd reason, I have this urge to connect the seven mortal sins to suicide; think about it: some of these sins or all of them can be cause for suicide. It sounds pathetic, but it's true. Let's go through it in no particular order:

1. PRIDE is defined as an excessive love of one's excellence or self-seeking or self-admiration; for me, this means that this person looks up

to his image so highly that everyone else is less of a person other than himself, for me everyone should be and need to be respected no matter what your status in life.

2. GREED: an inordinate or insatiable longing for material gain or excessive desire to accumulate large amounts of money; this word has a broad meaning. It can be defined in many different ways, but for me to define this, I would say a person who is longing for material things is willing to do an unspeakable act to hurt or even kill a person.

3. LUST refers to sex outside of marriage or enjoyment of sexual pleasure; I define this as a person that rapes a person against their will. I believe it's a mental and emotional sickness.

4. ENVY is a feeling of jealousy and wanting what someone else has or can do, or jealousy over the blessings and achievements of others; whenever I hear envy, I say admiration for that person who is blessed rather than be jealous or envy a person congratulate them for their success, and used that as an inspiration for yourself to succeed in life. I always say that I can't be the best in the world, but I can be the best of myself.

5. GLUTTONY is defined as overindulging in food or drinks or the overindulgence and overconsumption of anything to the point of waste. Does the word obesity and hoarding ring a bell? Whenever I hear this word, obesity and hoarding are not good words; we want to limit ourselves, especially regarding our health and personal belongings.

6. WRATH can be defined as uncontrolled feelings of anger, rage, and even hatred, or domestic violence, assault, road rage, terror attacks, and murder; I believe that pretty much sums up the definition of wrath, but whenever you are faced with such uncontrolled anger, take a deep breath and slowly exhale and repeat, and think that nothing good will come out of negative situations/emotions.

7. Lastly, SLOTH is defined as laziness, which is "without care," or a person not wanting to work because of their lack of motivation. For me, a sloth is a person who feeds or relies on other people's wealth or

success and makes that their own rather than work for themselves and earn for their keeps. It reminds me of that song by TLC, "No Scrubs."

The seven mortal sins, deeply rooted in the moral fabric of human existence, often reflect the struggles we encounter within ourselves and how they manifest in our actions, thoughts, and decisions. Pride, greed, lust, envy, gluttony, wrath, and sloth are not just abstract concepts but realities that many of us wrestle with daily. They embody the temptations, desires, and weaknesses that can lead us astray from a path of fulfillment, peace, and purpose. Each sin carries a weight, a consequence that reverberates through the choices we make and the lives we touch. When we think about these sins in the context of life's ultimate struggles, such as despair and, in extreme cases, suicide, we begin to see the profound impact they have on our mental and emotional well-being.

Pride, for instance, often starts as a harmless sense of self-worth but can evolve into an overwhelming obsession with one's image or status. It becomes a barrier, isolating individuals from meaningful connections and creating unrealistic expectations. This isolation can be devastating. Imagine a person who has built their entire identity around their success or reputation. When that identity is threatened—perhaps by failure, criticism, or rejection—the sense of loss can feel unbearable. This overwhelming fear of humiliation or exposure can lead to feelings of despair. Pride also prevents individuals from seeking help when they need it most. Admitting vulnerability requires humility, yet pride often silences that cry for support, leaving individuals to battle their demons alone. It is in this isolation that the seeds of hopelessness can grow.

Greed is another force that shapes human behavior in insidious ways. The insatiable longing for wealth, possessions, or power often blinds individuals to the value of what truly matters—relationships, love, and personal integrity. Greed drives a person to focus solely on acquiring more, often at the expense of their health, morals, and connections with others. The irony of greed is that it never truly satisfies. The pursuit of material wealth can create an empty void that nothing seems to fill. For those who base their worth on material success, financial failure or the realization that possessions cannot bring happiness can lead to a profound sense of emptiness. This can spiral into despair, particularly when the individual feels they have nothing else to offer or live for.

Lust, often trivialized in its portrayal, can have a deeply destructive impact on individuals and their relationships. At its core, lust objectifies and dehumanizes, reducing the sacred connection between people to a mere transaction or gratification. When left unchecked, it fosters behaviors that harm others, such as infidelity, exploitation, or even violence. The aftermath of acting on such impulses often leaves individuals feeling guilt, shame, and alienation. For those who fall victim to these acts, the trauma can be life-altering. The emotional scars of being used or abused can manifest as anxiety, depression, and in some cases, suicidal thoughts. Lust, when divorced from love and respect, leads to a cycle of harm and regret, diminishing the sense of worth and dignity of everyone involved.

Envy, perhaps one of the most relatable sins, is the quiet thief of joy. It creeps into the mind, convincing individuals that they are inadequate because they lack what others possess. This constant comparison to others—be it their achievements, possessions, or relationships—breeds dissatisfaction and resentment. Envy blinds individuals to their blessings and focuses their attention solely on what they lack. Over time, this can erode self-esteem and create a sense of failure. The belief that one can never measure up to others fosters hopelessness, particularly when coupled with the pressure to meet societal expectations. Instead of striving to improve, individuals consumed by envy may give up altogether, believing they are destined to fall short.

Gluttony, often associated solely with overeating, has broader implications that extend to overindulgence in any form. It represents a loss of control, where the pursuit of pleasure overtakes the discipline needed to maintain balance. Gluttony is not just about consumption but also about the emotional voids that individuals try to fill through excess. Whether it's food, alcohol, shopping, or other vices, overindulgence often masks deeper issues such as loneliness, stress, or unprocessed trauma. The consequences of gluttony—health problems, financial difficulties, or strained relationships—often lead to regret and self-loathing. The cycle of indulgence followed by guilt can create a downward spiral that leaves individuals feeling trapped and powerless to change.

Wrath is perhaps the most visible of the sins, manifesting as explosive anger, hatred, or violence. It is a force that destroys relationships, communities, and even the individual harboring it. Wrath blinds individuals to reason, leading them to act on impulses that they later regret. The aftermath of uncontrolled anger—be it a broken relationship, a physical altercation, or a loss of trust—often leaves a trail of destruction. For the individual, the weight of these actions can be crushing. Wrath turned inward, in the form of self-loathing or guilt, can be equally damaging. The inability to forgive oneself or others can lead to bitterness, isolation, and a sense of despair that becomes difficult to escape.

Finally, sloth, often dismissed as mere laziness, represents a deeper disengagement from life. It is the apathy that prevents individuals from pursuing their potential or finding meaning in their existence. Sloth is not just a lack of activity but a lack of purpose. When individuals lose their drive or motivation, they often retreat into themselves, avoiding responsibilities and connections with others. This detachment from life can lead to feelings of worthlessness and depression. Sloth creates a cycle of inaction that reinforces negative feelings, making it increasingly difficult to break free and find a sense of purpose.

The connection between these sins and the struggles that lead to despair, including suicidal thoughts, is not a condemnation but a reflection of how human vulnerabilities can spiral when left unaddressed. Each sin represents a part of the human experience—a desire, fear, or weakness that we all grapple with in different ways. The challenge lies in recognizing these tendencies within ourselves and addressing them before they take root and grow into something destructive.

What is most important to remember is that no sin, no struggle, and no darkness is insurmountable. The human capacity for growth, redemption, and transformation is extraordinary. While the seven mortal sins highlight the vulnerabilities we face, they also point to the virtues that can guide us toward a better path. Humility counters pride. Generosity replaces greed. Love transforms lust. Gratitude overcomes envy. Moderation balances gluttony. Forgiveness heals wrath. Purpose reignites sloth. By striving to cultivate these virtues, we can not only overcome our weaknesses but also create lives filled with meaning, connection, and joy.

For those who find themselves overwhelmed by the weight of these struggles, it is crucial to seek help and support. Whether through friends, family, faith, or professional guidance, reaching out can be the first step toward healing. It is a reminder that we are not alone in our battles and that there is always hope, even in the darkest moments. The seven mortal sins may represent the challenges we face, but they do not define us. What defines us is how we respond—our resilience, our willingness to grow, and our commitment to living lives of love, purpose, and grace.

MATURITY:

It is learning to walk away from people and situations threatening your peace of mind, self-respect, values, morals, or self-worth. It is also accepting responsibility whether we like it or not, when we were younger we take everything for granted, as if the things we have just appear out of nowhere, then as we grow older we soon found out that everything that we own from the food that we eat, water that we drink, clothes that we wear we have to work hard for it, we have to earn it. Maturity is about accepting life whether it is good or bad, hard or easy, we have to take into account the good from the bad and the bad to good. Maturity is acceptance but most importantly understanding. Understanding what is good for our self and to others. Maturity is learning what good, better is or best to succeed in life. Better to learn this early on in life rather than later, yourself and your love ones depends on it. Maturity grows as we age, it grows old as we grows old.

Maturity is a concept that touches every aspect of life, shaping how we relate to ourselves, others, and the world around us. It is a gradual process that goes beyond simply aging. While age is a natural factor in gaining maturity, the true essence of maturity comes from experience, reflection, and the lessons we learn along the way. It is an evolving state of being that requires us to grow, adapt, and understand both the good and the bad in life.

One of the first lessons of maturity is learning to walk away from people and situations that compromise our well-being. In our younger years, it's easy to stay attached to relationships or circumstances that drain us. We often remain in environments that threaten our peace of mind, our self-respect, or our core values because we fear change or we feel obligated. Maturity, however, teaches us that our mental and emotional health is paramount. It encourages us to assess the value of our relationships and situations, and to step away from what no longer serves our growth. It's not always easy, but it's necessary for maintaining inner peace and personal development.

Accepting responsibility is another hallmark of maturity. As children, we tend to take the things we have for granted, thinking that life simply provides for us. We rely on others to meet our needs without fully understanding the effort that goes into making things happen. It's only as we mature that we begin to appreciate the work, sacrifices, and decisions that contribute to our lives. The food we eat, the water we drink, and the clothes we wear are not just things that magically appear—they are the result of hard work, planning, and the efforts of others. Maturity teaches us to appreciate the world around us and acknowledge the efforts that go into providing for us. Moreover, it pushes us to take ownership of our own lives, making conscious choices and facing the consequences of those choices.

Maturity also involves learning to accept life as it is, with all its ups and downs. The notion of life being a mixture of both good and bad is a critical part of maturity. We often expect life to be easy, to be filled with constant joy and satisfaction, but as we grow older, we realize that life is unpredictable. It can be difficult and challenging, but it can also be rewarding and beautiful. Maturity involves understanding that there will always be obstacles, setbacks, and moments of hardship, but there will also be joy, love, and growth. The key is to find balance, to learn from each experience, and to recognize that each phase of life offers valuable lessons. Even in our darkest moments, there is wisdom to be gained if we are open to learning from them.

Equally important to maturity is understanding what is truly good for ourselves and others. It's not just about making decisions based on what feels good in the moment, but about considering the long-term impact of our actions. Maturity teaches us the value of self-awareness and empathy. We learn to distinguish between what is merely pleasing and what is truly beneficial for our well-being. We also learn to consider how our actions affect the people around us. Understanding the needs, feelings, and perspectives of others is a critical part of maturity, and it fosters healthier, more compassionate relationships. It allows us to navigate the complexities of human interactions with greater sensitivity and respect.

In addition to understanding what is good for ourselves, maturity teaches us to recognize what is better and what is best. This growth in discernment is essential for success in life. The path to success is often paved with choices, and not all of them are easy. It's easy to get distracted by short-term desires or impulsive decisions, but maturity teaches us to consider the long-term consequences of our actions. Maturity helps us choose wisely, prioritizing what is truly important and aligning our choices with our values. Learning what is better or best requires patience, reflection, and the ability to delay gratification in favor of more meaningful, sustainable success. It's a skill that develops over time, often through trial and error, but it's essential for building a fulfilling and purposeful life.

Maturity is a lifelong process that continues to evolve as we grow older. It's not something we simply reach at a certain age or stage of life, but rather something that deepens and expands with each passing year. The more we experience, the more we learn about ourselves, about others, and about the world around us. Each stage of life brings new challenges, but also new opportunities for growth. Maturity, therefore, is not about perfection, but about the willingness to embrace change and to learn from every experience. It's about becoming more grounded in our values, more compassionate towards others, and more aware of our place in the world.

The growth of maturity is also tied to the people we surround ourselves with and the lessons they impart. The relationships we form, the mentors we seek, and the communities we join all contribute to our personal development. We learn from the experiences and wisdom of others, and in turn, we share our own insights. This exchange of knowledge and understanding is vital to our growth. Sometimes, we need the support of others to help us navigate difficult decisions or to remind us of our own worth when we forget. It's important to recognize that maturity is not just about personal reflection and growth, but also about engaging with the world and others in meaningful ways.

While maturity can sometimes be a difficult and slow process, it is ultimately one of the most rewarding journeys of our lives. It enables us to lead lives that are more fulfilling, authentic, and aligned with our true selves. It allows us to face life's challenges with resilience and to make choices that are rooted in wisdom and compassion. Maturity is the key to finding balance in a world that is constantly changing, and it empowers us to be our best selves, not only for our own benefit but for the benefit of others as well.

One of the first steps in maturity is understanding that life doesn't always unfold as we expect or hope. We grow up with ideas of how things should be—our plans, goals, and dreams—and we often have this illusion of control. Yet maturity teaches us that while we can make plans and set goals, the outcome may not always be what we envisioned. It is about embracing uncertainty and being prepared to adjust when things don't go according to plan. This doesn't mean giving up on one's ambitions or becoming passive, but rather understanding that life's flow sometimes requires flexibility, patience, and adaptability. The willingness to accept the unexpected is a mark of maturity, as it enables us to move forward with grace when things change beyond our control.

A key component of maturity is emotional intelligence. When we are younger, we may find it challenging to understand our own feelings, let alone the feelings of others. However, maturity encourages us to reflect on our emotions and the emotions of the people around us. This awareness helps us build deeper and more meaningful relationships. We learn to listen attentively, not just to respond but to understand the underlying emotions at play. We also begin to recognize that everyone is fighting their own battles, and we develop empathy, which allows us to connect with others on a more human level.

The development of emotional intelligence also involves learning how to handle negative emotions such as anger, fear, or frustration. These feelings are natural, but maturity is the ability to channel these emotions in healthy and productive ways. Instead of lashing out, a mature person takes a step back, evaluates the situation, and reacts thoughtfully. This process requires self-control and patience, as well as the realization that our emotions don't define us; it's how we handle them that shapes who we are. Moreover, maturity helps us to better understand how our actions, driven by these emotions, can impact others. This mindfulness ensures we act in ways that align with our values and not just in reaction to external triggers.

Moreover, maturity calls for a deeper understanding of relationships and their complexities. At a younger age, relationships often seem straightforward—they are either good or bad, simple or complicated. But as we grow, we realize that relationships are dynamic and multifaceted. They require effort, communication, and mutual respect. We learn that it's not enough to simply "like" someone or have a shared connection; instead, we must also nurture the relationship by being honest, being present, and being kind. This doesn't mean that every relationship will thrive, but maturity gives us the tools to recognize when it's time to let go of toxic relationships or work to improve others. We come to understand the importance of quality over quantity in friendships and the value of having a few deep, supportive relationships rather than many superficial ones.

Another important aspect of maturity is the ability to prioritize long-term well-being over short-term pleasure. Youth is often associated with a desire for immediate gratification—whether it's through material possessions, experiences, or indulgence. While there's nothing wrong with enjoying life in the present, maturity encourages us to recognize the importance of delayed gratification. It's about making choices today that will positively impact our future selves. This could involve setting aside money for savings, investing time in relationships, or dedicating ourselves to self-improvement. It's the understanding that the actions we take now ripple into the future, shaping the quality of life we will lead. As we mature, we begin to take our long-term health—both physical and emotional—into account. The desire for instant rewards gives way to the fulfillment that comes from long-term efforts.

At the core of maturity is the realization that we are all connected, and that the well-being of others plays a crucial role in our own. It's easy to get caught up in our own struggles, particularly when we are navigating personal difficulties or pursuing our own goals. But maturity teaches us that our actions impact others, and by helping others succeed or by simply being kind, we contribute to a greater sense of community and fulfillment. Whether it's offering support to a friend in need, donating to a cause we care about, or taking part in something that helps the broader community, maturity acknowledges the value in collective efforts. We move beyond a self-centered existence toward one that is guided by a broader sense of responsibility for the world around us.

Furthermore, maturity requires resilience—the ability to persevere in the face of setbacks and failure. Life is full of ups and downs, and there will be times when things don't go as planned, or when we face personal or professional failures. Maturity doesn't involve avoiding failure, but rather accepting that it is part of the learning process. When we fall, we get back up; when we fail, we learn from our mistakes. Resilience allows us to adapt to life's challenges and to keep moving forward with a sense of hope and determination. Maturity teaches us that it's not how many times we fall, but how we rise and what we learn along the way that truly matters.

Another profound aspect of maturity is the ability to set healthy boundaries. As we grow, we become increasingly aware of what we need in order to thrive—whether it's space for self-care, time for reflection, or distance from toxic relationships. Setting boundaries can be one of the hardest aspects of maturity, as it often involves saying "no" to others in order to preserve our own well-being. Yet, this is a crucial skill to develop, as it empowers us to protect our energy and focus on what truly matters. It allows us to build healthier relationships by ensuring that we aren't overextending ourselves or compromising our values for the sake of others. Through this process, we learn that setting boundaries isn't selfish, but an essential part of living authentically.

One of the final hallmarks of maturity is the ability to embrace vulnerability. As we mature, we learn that vulnerability is not a weakness, but a strength. It's the courage to show up authentically, to express our true feelings, and to allow ourselves to be seen without pretense. It's through vulnerability that we build the deepest connections with others, because it allows for true intimacy. It's also through vulnerability that we find our greatest strength, as we become more resilient, compassionate, and self-aware. Embracing vulnerability means acknowledging our imperfections and being open to learning, growing, and evolving as individuals.

Maturity does not happen overnight—it is an ongoing journey of growth and self-discovery. It requires patience, resilience, and a willingness to reflect on our experiences. As we mature, we learn to navigate the complexities of life with greater ease, understanding, and grace. We develop the emotional intelligence to navigate relationships, the resilience to overcome challenges, and the wisdom to make decisions that align with our values. Maturity enriches our lives, providing us with the tools to face whatever comes our way, while also helping us contribute to the well-being of those around us. It is through this continuous process of growth and self-awareness that we become the best version of ourselves.

ANGER:

REE THREE MINI'S:

Lately, I have been mentally mad, mad about nothing; I believe I have been watching a lot of negativity on television, which is affecting my mental health. I felt emotionally in rage over nothing, and I'm not hurting anyone. It's just the feeling I have inside. So I needed soul searching: what is happening inside me? Why am I thinking this way? I am not misbehaving or acting it out; it's just my mental emotion; that negative feeling are creeping up on me, and I know it's wrong. I need to find a way to disrupt or cut off this feeling. I wouldn't say I liked it because I felt like a ticking bomb ready to explode any time now. So I pray, I pray line. I know how to pray for guidance to shake off this negative feeling. And so my inner voice told me to stop watching violent TV shows that are corrupting my brain. And it works! The things surrounding you can indeed affect thoughts and emotions. So, I need to detach or refrain my self from watching shows on TV that are affecting my mental health. I guess this is not far off from being influenced by social media; if you listen long enough to this person (the influencer), you would believe that what they are saying is accurate, and some of us believe it so much that some goes into that rabbit hole and can't dig themselves out of it (or gotten so immerse to it), I remember way back when internet wasn't a thing, my influencer are my family, my cousin, friends, classmates in school, my mom and dad, my older half brother. I look up to them for the great things they do, not for the great things they do that also teach me a great lesson in life. For those who are reading this, remember this: when you do bad things, bad things will happen to you, but when you do good things, good things will happen. No evil deeds are left unpunished. Your brain is the captain of your ship (your body) ever. Your mind says your body will follow. Put away all that negativity from your mind and think of positive thoughts; positive things will happen to you.

Anger is a complex and often misunderstood emotion. It's something that many of us experience from time to time, but when it becomes a persistent and overwhelming feeling, it can take a toll on our mental and emotional well-being. It is not always easy to understand the roots of this anger or where it comes from, especially when it seems to emerge from nowhere. As you mentioned, this sense of rage can sometimes feel irrational, affecting us deeply even when there's no obvious cause. It's a feeling that can be challenging to express, and when it remains internalized, it can feel like a ticking bomb ready to explode.

In your reflection, you've done something very important: you've acknowledged the anger and taken steps toward understanding its source. The first step in addressing any emotion is recognizing it for what it is, rather than dismissing it or pretending it doesn't exist. By being honest with yourself about the anger you're experiencing, you're already on the path to healing and resolution. Your search for the underlying cause of your anger is a key part of emotional growth. Emotions don't arise in a vacuum; they are often the result of deeper, sometimes subconscious, factors.

One of the things you identified was the negative influence of the media, particularly violent television shows. It's a powerful insight that what we consume mentally can directly affect our emotional state. Our brains are constantly absorbing information, whether we realize it or not, and when that information is filled with negativity, it can impact how we think and feel. The images, stories, and messages we are exposed to shape our perceptions of the world, often reinforcing fear, anger, and anxiety. When we spend too much time immersing ourselves in violent or upsetting content, it can alter our mood and behavior without us even noticing. It's no surprise that cutting off this type of content had a positive impact on your mental state. This is a reminder of the importance of being mindful about what we choose to let into our lives, whether it's through television, social media, or even the people we surround ourselves with.

Taking control of the things that influence your thoughts and emotions is one of the most powerful tools you have in managing your mental health. This awareness of the connection between media consumption and emotional well-being is not just relevant in relation to television; it extends to social media, news outlets, and other forms of communication. As you pointed out, the influence of online personalities or influencers can be incredibly powerful. Their words and actions can shape our thoughts, beliefs, and attitudes, sometimes without us even realizing it. This is why it's so important to question what we hear and see, to verify information, and to ensure that the voices we allow into our minds are positive and uplifting, rather than toxic and harmful.

Your example of family members being your influencers in the past offers an interesting contrast. Before the rise of the internet, people primarily learned from those around them, from parents, relatives, teachers, and friends. These relationships were more personal, and the lessons learned were often grounded in lived experiences and genuine care. In today's digital age, we face an overwhelming amount of information from people who may not know us personally, and who may not have our best interests at heart. In some ways, it's much harder to discern what is worth absorbing and what is harmful. This is why, just as you learned from those who had a positive influence in your life, it's essential to carefully curate the content we engage with today.

Your reflections also touch on an important life lesson: the principle of cause and effect. You wisely noted that when we engage in bad actions, we invite negative consequences, and conversely, when we choose to do good, we invite positive outcomes. This is not just a moral principle, but also a psychological truth. The actions we take shape our lives, and often, the way we act towards others will be reflected back to us. If we act with kindness, integrity, and respect, we are more likely to attract the same qualities from those around us. On the other hand, when we harbor anger, resentment, or negativity, we tend to find more of those qualities in our lives as well. It's a simple yet profound truth that underscores the importance of mindfulness in our actions, words, and thoughts.

Another key point you raised was about the power of the mind. As you said, "Your brain is the captain of your ship," and indeed, this is a powerful truth. Our minds direct our actions, and how we think about the world will determine how we experience it. If we allow negativity to dominate our thoughts, it will shape our reality in negative ways. But when we choose to focus on positivity, gratitude, and growth, our reality begins to reflect those qualities as well. The mind is incredibly powerful in this way, and the more we learn to harness its strength, the more control we have over our emotional and mental state.

One way to cultivate this positive mindset is through practices like mindfulness and meditation. These tools allow us to become more aware of our thoughts, emotions, and the triggers that set them off. When we can observe our thoughts without judgment, we gain the ability to choose which ones to engage with and which ones to let go. This practice of detaching from negative thoughts is an essential step in reclaiming our mental health and emotional well-being. Over time, mindfulness can help us build emotional resilience, making it easier to stay calm in stressful situations and less susceptible to the influence of external negativity.

Another way to shift our mindset is through gratitude. When we focus on the things we are grateful for, we begin to shift our attention away from what is lacking or negative in our lives. Gratitude helps to rewire the brain, strengthening positive pathways and reducing the power of negative thoughts. It's a practice that can be done daily, even if it's just taking a moment to reflect on the small things that bring us joy and peace. Over time, gratitude can create a powerful shift in how we view ourselves, our circumstances, and the world around us.

Your reflections on anger, media influence, and the power of the mind offer valuable insights into how we can take control of our emotional well-being. By being mindful of the content we consume, the people we surround ourselves with, and the thoughts we entertain, we can create a more positive mental environment. It's important to remember that emotions, even negative ones, are a natural part of the human experience. But by taking responsibility for our mental state, engaging in practices that foster positivity, and living with integrity, we can cultivate a sense of peace and emotional balance. As you wisely said, "Put away all that negativity from your mind, and think of positive thoughts; positive things will happen to you." This is not just a hopeful belief, but a powerful truth that can guide us toward a healthier, more fulfilling life.

Anger is a powerful and often overwhelming emotion, one that can arise for reasons both clear and unclear. It can be an intense feeling that swells within, creating a sense of inner turmoil that disrupts peace of mind. For many people, this emotion seems to come out of nowhere, triggering a sense of frustration and helplessness, especially when it feels like the source of the anger cannot be easily identified. Understanding why anger manifests can be one of the first steps toward overcoming it, as it allows us to better manage and cope with such emotions.

In your reflection, you discussed a powerful realization about the impact of external influences on your emotional state. You recognized that watching negative or violent content on television was contributing to your feelings of rage, and by stepping away from that kind of programming, you were able to regain control of your emotions. This is an essential insight into how much power the external world has over our internal world. Our emotions are not isolated from the world around us. In fact, they are often directly influenced by the content we consume—whether that's through media, social interactions, or the environments we place ourselves in.

We are bombarded daily by external stimuli that can stir up emotions, thoughts, and feelings. The information we consume is far from neutral—it carries with it messages, tones, and biases that shape how we see the world. Negative content, such as violent television shows or news about tragedy and hardship, can heighten our stress levels, increase feelings of helplessness, and even reinforce a sense of anger toward the world around us. The more we are exposed to such content, the more we might start internalizing these negative emotions, which can affect our mental health and well-being.

But recognizing that this is happening is half the battle. By consciously choosing what we allow into our lives, we gain more control over our emotional state. It's easy to feel powerless when anger takes over, but as you've demonstrated, we have the power to disrupt those feelings. Shifting away from negative media is a practical and powerful tool in taking back control of our mental and emotional health. We can replace it with more positive content, things that bring joy, understanding, and peace into our lives, whether that's through inspiring stories, uplifting music, or educational material that broadens our understanding of the world in a healthy way.

Social media, much like television, can also have a profound impact on our emotional state. In recent years, the rise of social media influencers has introduced an entirely new dynamic to how we consume information and how we allow it to shape our thinking. Influencers are people who have gained significant followings on various platforms, using their popularity to promote ideas, products, or lifestyles. While there is much positive content shared by influencers, there is also a great deal of negativity, superficiality, and misinformation that can seep into our lives. The constant exposure to filtered images, unrealistic expectations, and biased opinions can lead to feelings of inadequacy, frustration, and anger, particularly if we begin comparing our lives to the highly curated versions that influencers present.

It's important to approach social media with a sense of awareness, understanding that not everything we see online is a true reflection of reality. The people we follow on these platforms, while often charismatic and persuasive, are not immune to their own struggles and challenges. Many influencers only show a polished version of their lives, which can create unrealistic expectations. This distorted view can lead to a sense of frustration, anger, or disappointment, especially when we feel like our own lives don't measure up.

The key to navigating this world is discernment. As with television, we have to be mindful of who we allow to influence our thoughts and emotions. We must also learn to filter out negativity, avoiding content that fuels anger or dissatisfaction. This practice of mindful consumption extends to our interactions with others as well. Just as we filter the media we consume, we should also consider the people we allow into our lives. Negative or toxic relationships can have an equally harmful impact on our emotional health, contributing to feelings of anger, resentment, or bitterness.

You also touched on an important concept in your reflection: the idea that the people we look up to—our influencers—have always played a significant role in shaping our thoughts and actions. Before the rise of social media and television, our primary sources of influence came from our immediate circle: family, friends, and peers. The lessons we learned from them were deeply personal and rooted in real-life experiences. The people we admired often played a direct role in shaping our values, choices, and perspectives.

The shift to online influencers, however, has introduced new complexities. While social media gives us access to a wider range of perspectives and insights, it also exposes us to a greater diversity of opinions, many of which may not align with our own values or beliefs. It becomes easy to get lost in the vast sea of information and fall into the trap of believing that we must align ourselves with the voices that dominate the conversation. But just as you've acknowledged, it's important to remember that when we look up to someone, we are not just admiring their outward accomplishments—we are also internalizing their beliefs, values, and perspectives.

The people we look up to should inspire us to be better, not fuel negative emotions or reinforce destructive behaviors. It's crucial that we choose our role models carefully, ensuring that the voices we allow to influence us are rooted in positivity, growth, and authenticity. Our choices in this regard will directly affect how we feel about ourselves and the world around us.

Your reflection also touched on a profound life principle: the idea that actions have consequences, and those consequences—whether positive or negative—are a reflection of the energy we put into the world. The concept of cause and effect is not just an abstract idea; it is deeply embedded in the fabric of our lives. When we engage in positive actions, we invite more positivity into our lives. Similarly, negative actions often lead to negative outcomes. This is not just a moral lesson—it's a psychological truth. Our thoughts, words, and actions create a ripple effect in the world around us, and that ripple will eventually return to us.

By choosing to focus on positivity, kindness, and gratitude, we can begin to shift the energy we put into the world. When we make the effort to do good, not just for ourselves but for others, we create a cycle of positivity that continues to grow. This is one of the most empowering aspects of life: we have the ability to choose the kind of energy we bring into the world, and in doing so, we can create a life that reflects the values we hold dear.

In closing, your reflections on anger, media influence, and the importance of choosing our influences carefully offer valuable insights into managing emotions and cultivating a more peaceful and positive life. While it's natural to experience anger from time to time, it's how we respond to it that makes all the difference. By becoming more mindful of the content we consume, the people we allow to influence us, and the actions we take, we can create an environment—both internal and external—that nurtures peace, understanding, and growth. The more we practice this mindfulness, the more we can reduce the impact of negativity in our lives and replace it with positive, life-affirming energy.

One of the most pervasive sources of negativity in modern life is media. Television shows, news outlets, and even social media are often saturated with violence, drama, and distressing content. While these mediums are designed to entertain or inform, they often do so in ways that focus on the more negative aspects of life. This is especially true for programs that center on conflict, injustice, or violence. The constant exposure to this type of content can have a numbing effect on the viewer's emotional state, desensitizing them to real-world problems and, in some cases, even triggering feelings of anger or helplessness.

Your realization that violent television shows were affecting your mental health is a profound insight. This recognition shows an important step toward emotional maturity—understanding that we are not passive consumers of content but active participants in how it shapes our emotional and mental well-being. By choosing to step away from programs that breed negativity, you have taken an essential first step in taking control of your emotional health. It is a reminder that we can actively curate the content we consume and that we have the power to walk away from things that threaten our peace of mind.

This concept of controlling external influences is not limited to media. Social media, for example, has become an even more pervasive source of negativity in many people's lives. Platforms like Instagram, Twitter, and Facebook are filled with highly curated images of other people's lives, often presenting a distorted or unrealistic version of reality. The constant comparison to others can lead to feelings of inadequacy, jealousy, and frustration. It's easy to fall into the trap of measuring our self-worth against the seemingly perfect lives of others, but this comparison is rarely helpful and almost always damaging.

When we spend too much time on social media, we often see only the best moments of others' lives—the vacations, the accomplishments, the beautiful photos. What's often missing from these depictions are the struggles, the failures, and the real-life challenges that everyone faces. Yet, when we only see one side of the story, it can be easy to believe that everyone else has it together while we are struggling to keep up. This can exacerbate feelings of anger, resentment, or frustration with ourselves or the world around us.

It's important to remember that social media, like television, is a curated experience. It's not an accurate reflection of reality. We must be mindful of how much time we spend consuming this content and recognize when it begins to negatively affect our emotional state. The same way you took the initiative to stop watching violent TV shows, we can choose to spend less time on social media or unfollow accounts that trigger negative emotions. Instead, we can fill our feeds with positive influences—accounts that inspire us, that offer real, unfiltered glimpses into people's lives, and that promote self-care and healthy living.

The idea of external influences shaping our emotional world extends to the people we surround ourselves with. Sometimes, without even realizing it, we allow toxic relationships to seep into our lives, contributing to feelings of anger and frustration. Toxic relationships can take many forms, whether that's a friend who constantly drains your energy with negativity, a family member who undermines your self-esteem, or a coworker who engages in gossip or drama. These relationships can have a profound effect on how we feel about ourselves and the world around us. The emotions we experience in these interactions—frustration, anger, sadness—are not always a reflection of who we are but of the environment that has been created by these toxic people.

Just as we have the power to choose the content we consume, we also have the power to choose who we allow into our lives. The people we surround ourselves with can either lift us up or bring us down, and it's crucial to make conscious decisions about the relationships we invest in. While it's not always easy to distance ourselves from people who are negative or harmful, doing so is essential for protecting our peace of mind.

Healthy relationships are those that encourage growth, understanding, and mutual respect. These relationships provide a sense of safety, where we feel valued, heard, and supported. They nurture our emotional well-being and contribute to a positive mental environment. When we surround ourselves with people who share our values, support our goals, and promote positivity, we are more likely to feel balanced and centered, even in challenging times. On the other hand, toxic relationships drain our energy, reinforce negative thought patterns, and keep us stuck in cycles of anger, frustration, and resentment.

The importance of surrounding ourselves with positive influences extends to our self-talk as well. Often, we are our own worst critics, filling our minds with negative thoughts and doubts. This inner dialogue can be just as harmful, if not more so, than the external influences we face. Negative self-talk can undermine our confidence, increase feelings of anger, and perpetuate a cycle of self-loathing. However, just as we can change the external content we consume, we can also change the way we speak to ourselves. By practicing self-compassion and positive affirmations, we can shift our internal narrative to one that is more empowering and supportive.

Another important realization in your reflection is the concept of responsibility. You touched on the idea that when we are younger, we tend to take everything for granted. We don't fully appreciate the effort and work that goes into providing for ourselves and others. However, as we grow older, we come to realize that the things we have in life—food, water, shelter—are not automatic; they are the result of hard work, sacrifice, and responsibility. This is a significant aspect of maturity—the ability to take ownership of our lives and actions.

As we mature, we learn that anger, when left unchecked, can prevent us from moving forward in a healthy and productive way. It becomes a barrier that keeps us from accepting responsibility and finding constructive solutions to our challenges. Learning to manage anger and channel it in productive ways is a sign of emotional maturity. This is not to say that we should suppress our feelings; rather, we should learn how to express them in ways that are respectful and productive. Taking responsibility for our emotions, actions, and the consequences of our decisions is a key component of personal growth.

In summary, the journey of managing anger and negative emotions is one of awareness, responsibility, and intentionality. By recognizing the external influences that affect our emotions—whether that's through media, relationships, or self-talk—we can take steps to create a more positive and balanced emotional environment. The choices we make, the people we surround ourselves with, and the way we treat ourselves all contribute to our overall mental and emotional well-being. As we grow older and become more aware of these influences, we gain the power to create a life that is centered on peace, understanding, and growth.

HAPPINESS:

What makes a person happy? We should ask ourselves this question. Sometimes, we look so far ahead of ourselves that we miss the things right before us; everyone has our happiness. A friend of mine said that he loved to go fishing, and it made me wonder how I never really asked anyone what was happening in life? It's a simple question, yet it is often ignored. Personally, what makes me happy? Count how I love listening to music, especially when I'm alone, in the bathroom, driving, walking, or running. I love to sing, despite not having a good voice, I still love to sing; it is one of my happy moments. Also, watching movies, and television series keeps me entertained. I love to exercise because it keeps me healthy and agile. Working on my ligaments and muscles keeps my heart pumping, and I love to run. And yes, I love to work, to go to my job, because it pays my bills and keeps a roof above my head. I am grateful to be working for the government because my job keeps the public safe, so not only do I help people, but I also enjoy doing what

I do. In addition, I love my family, my wife, and my kids. They bring joy and self-accomplishment to me; they are my world. I love little things in life; I love praying every day to be grateful for all the blessings I receive, big or small. I don't complain much about life; I try to adapt to all life experiences. I try not to worry about the things that I cannot control, rather focusing on myself to be a better person from yesterday, and tomorrow. These are some of the things that make me happy. What is yours?

Happiness is an elusive and deeply personal concept. It's something that often varies greatly from person to person, shaped by individual experiences, values, and desires. The question of what truly makes a person happy is worth reflecting on, and it's important to regularly ask ourselves this question. In doing so, we may discover that our sources of happiness are often simpler and closer than we think. Sometimes, in our search for happiness, we look too far ahead or get caught up in the pursuit of grand goals, only to miss the little joys right in front of us.

For some, happiness is found in solitude, in moments of quiet reflection and personal space. For example, one of your friends finds joy in fishing, an activity that many might see as quiet or solitary, but which brings them peace and contentment. It serves as a reminder that happiness can come from the simplest of activities, and that we should take time to appreciate the small moments that fill our days. It's easy to forget, in the hustle and bustle of life, that we all have our own unique sources of happiness, sometimes right under our noses.

In your reflection, you highlight several aspects of your life that bring you happiness. Music, for example, plays a crucial role in your life. The ability to listen to music anytime—whether you're alone, in the car, or even while running—offers a sense of connection to your emotions and the world around you. Music has a powerful effect on the mind, often serving as a form of therapy. It can uplift our spirits, calm our anxieties, or even provide a much-needed escape from the stresses of life. Singing, even without the "perfect" voice, is another form of personal expression that adds to the joy you find in life. Sometimes, it's not about having a beautiful voice but about the joy of doing something that makes us feel alive and free.

Television, movies, and TV series are another part of your happiness. Entertainment is an essential part of life, giving us a chance to relax, unwind, and experience different worlds. The ability to lose yourself in a good story, whether through laughter or tears, offers a break from daily challenges and allows for a fresh perspective. The power of storytelling has been around for centuries, and it remains one of the most accessible ways to find joy and connection in an often overwhelming world.

Exercise, too, is a significant source of happiness for you. The physical activity that keeps you healthy also contributes to your mental well-being. Whether it's working on your ligaments and muscles or simply running to get your heart pumping, exercise has a multitude of benefits. Not only does it improve your physical health, but it also releases endorphins—the body's natural mood boosters. Physical activity provides a sense of accomplishment, strength, and vitality that contributes to overall happiness. Staying active also gives you the energy and mindset to take on the day, helping to combat stress and anxiety.

Your love for your work is another profound source of happiness. The fact that your job allows you to contribute to the safety and well-being of others brings a sense of purpose. You don't just work to pay the bills, but you do so with a sense of pride, knowing that your efforts have a positive impact on the community. Having a job that aligns with your values can bring immense satisfaction, and this sense of fulfillment often leads to a greater sense of happiness in life. Many people find joy not in the paycheck, but in the knowledge that they are doing meaningful work, helping others, and contributing to society in a way that matters.

Your family, too, is at the heart of your happiness. The love you have for your wife and children is a constant source of joy and self-accomplishment. Family relationships provide a unique kind of support that no other aspect of life can replicate. Your family is a source of unconditional love and encouragement, offering a sense of grounding and belonging. Watching your children grow, experiencing their milestones, and being part of their lives brings fulfillment. The joy of being a part of something greater than yourself—the love, the laughter, the shared moments of connection—forms a core part of your happiness.

You also mention the importance of gratitude and prayer. In practicing gratitude, you take a moment every day to acknowledge the blessings in your life, both big and small. Gratitude allows you to shift your focus away from what you don't have, and instead, appreciate the wealth of blessings that are already present. Whether it's the warmth of a family dinner, the beauty of a quiet sunset, or the comfort of your own home, practicing gratitude brings peace and contentment. Prayer, as part of this gratitude practice, serves as a reminder of your connection to something greater than yourself—whether that's a higher power, the universe, or simply the flow of life. It can bring clarity, comfort, and a deep sense of inner peace.

One of the most important aspects of happiness, as you touch upon, is the ability to adapt. Life doesn't always go as planned, and there are times when things are beyond our control. In these moments, the ability to accept what is and adapt to the circumstances can be transformative. By focusing on what we can control—our actions, our mindset, and our attitude—we can find contentment even in difficult situations. Rather than dwelling on what is out of our hands, we learn to flow with life, knowing that each challenge is an opportunity to grow and evolve.

Happiness, at its core, is a combination of simple joys and deeper sense of purpose. It's about finding joy in everyday moments—whether that's through music, exercise, family, or work—and also embracing a mindset of gratitude, adaptability, and self-awareness. The happiness you describe in your reflection isn't tied to material possessions or fleeting pleasures but is rooted in the things that matter most: connection, purpose, and well-being.

In thinking about your own sources of happiness, it's important to ask: what makes me happy? It's a question worth revisiting often, as life changes and our priorities evolve. Sometimes happiness can be found in new hobbies, in the people we meet, or in different experiences. The key, however, is to remain open to the small moments that bring joy, and to cultivate a mindset that appreciates the richness of life.

For those who may be struggling to identify what makes them happy, it's worth exploring what brings a sense of peace and contentment. Whether that's through connecting with loved ones, pursuing a passion, engaging in self-care, or contributing to the well-being of others, happiness is a journey that is deeply personal. We all have different paths to follow, but the common thread is the pursuit of peace, joy, and fulfillment.

Ultimately, the secret to happiness may not lie in grand achievements or external circumstances, but in the small, consistent practices that bring us joy, peace, and a sense of meaning. In embracing these moments, we find that happiness is not a destination but a journey, one that we can create for ourselves with intention and gratitude.

Happiness is often considered the ultimate goal of human existence. It's the feeling of joy and contentment that people seek throughout their lives, yet it can sometimes feel elusive. Many chase happiness through wealth, fame, or external accomplishments, but true happiness often comes from within. It is about the simple things that we experience on a daily basis—things that are sometimes easy to overlook in our fast-paced, goal-driven society.

One important realization is that happiness is not a static state, but a dynamic one. It changes depending on where we are in life, the people we are surrounded by, and the choices we make. What makes one person happy might not make another person feel the same way, and that's okay. Happiness is personal, and its definition evolves as we grow, learn, and adapt. It's crucial, then, to not only understand what makes us happy but also to allow ourselves the flexibility to change that understanding as we progress through different stages of life.

For some, happiness might be deeply rooted in a sense of purpose or achievement. Accomplishments can give us a sense of satisfaction and pride. It's easy to feel accomplished after completing a challenging project at work or finishing a task that required effort and perseverance. But the satisfaction of accomplishment can be fleeting if we focus solely on achievements and not on the process itself. True happiness doesn't just come from crossing things off a to-do list; it comes from engaging in the process with purpose, enjoying the journey, and finding meaning in every step.

Another aspect that contributes to happiness is the ability to form meaningful connections with others. Relationships—whether with family, friends, or romantic partners—are a central source of joy for many people. The simple act of spending quality time with loved ones can bring immense satisfaction. It's often not the material gifts or grand gestures that make a relationship special, but the moments of shared laughter, empathy, and support. True happiness can be found in these everyday interactions, where the love and understanding between individuals create a sense of belonging and security.

Spending time with family or close friends allows us to reconnect with our true selves. These relationships offer a safe space for vulnerability, where we can express our fears, dreams, and frustrations without fear of judgment. It's in these moments of honest exchange that we experience emotional fulfillment. The bond that is built through years of shared experiences—whether they are moments of joy or times of hardship—shapes us in profound ways and contributes to a deep sense of well-being.

It's also important to recognize that happiness is often rooted in gratitude. When we appreciate the things we have—our health, our relationships, our homes, our work—we cultivate an internal sense of peace that can be incredibly fulfilling. Too often, we focus on what we don't have, constantly striving for the next big thing. However, when we take the time to acknowledge the blessings already present in our lives, we realize that we have more than enough to be content.

Gratitude shifts our perspective from scarcity to abundance, and this shift can profoundly affect our overall happiness.

For instance, taking a moment every day to reflect on what you are grateful for can lead to a more positive mindset. It might be something as simple as appreciating the beauty of a sunrise or the comforting embrace of a loved one. This small act of gratitude can help us feel more present and attuned to the goodness in our lives. It's an ongoing practice that can make a significant difference in how we experience the world.

The concept of mindfulness also plays a critical role in happiness. Being mindful means being fully present in the moment and aware of our thoughts, feelings, and sensations without judgment. This practice can help reduce stress and anxiety, as it encourages us to accept life as it is, rather than constantly striving for something else. By embracing mindfulness, we open ourselves up to the beauty of the present moment, free from the worries and distractions that often cloud our happiness.

It's also worth mentioning that happiness is not an emotion that we can always control. It's natural for us to experience negative emotions such as sadness, anger, or fear. These emotions are part of being human, and it's important to allow ourselves to feel them. In fact, it's through experiencing a full range of emotions that we can better appreciate the moments of happiness when they arise. Emotions are not enemies to be feared but signals that guide us toward what we need. Sometimes, the most profound moments of growth come from experiencing sadness or frustration, as they allow us to reassess our priorities and values.

Happiness is also linked to a sense of self-acceptance. In a world that often encourages us to compare ourselves to others, it can be difficult to appreciate our own unique qualities. However, true happiness comes from embracing who we are, with all our strengths and flaws. When we stop measuring our worth against external standards and start recognizing our inherent value, we become more at peace with ourselves. This acceptance enables us to cultivate self-love, which is foundational to happiness. It allows us to move through life with confidence, knowing that we are enough just as we are.

Moreover, cultivating a sense of purpose can lead to lasting happiness. People who have a clear sense of purpose—whether it's through their work, their passions, or their desire to make a difference in the world—tend to experience greater fulfillment. Purpose provides direction and meaning, making life feel more intentional. It offers a sense of accomplishment that is not dependent on external validation, but rather on the inner satisfaction of knowing that we are contributing to something greater than ourselves.

Finding purpose often requires self-reflection. It may involve asking ourselves difficult questions: What do I care about? What are my values? What do I want to achieve in life? This process can take time, and the answers may not always be clear. However, once we begin to align our actions with our values and passions, we begin to feel a sense of purpose that deeply enriches our lives.

Another important factor to consider when thinking about happiness is the role of resilience. Life is full of challenges, and how we respond to them can significantly impact our happiness. Resilience is the ability to bounce back from adversity, to keep moving forward even when faced with obstacles. Resilient people are not immune to hardship, but they have developed coping mechanisms that help them navigate difficult situations. By cultivating resilience, we learn to see challenges as opportunities for growth rather than insurmountable roadblocks. This mindset shift can foster a greater sense of control over our lives, which contributes to our happiness.

It's also helpful to recognize that happiness is often linked to the ability to let go. Sometimes, we hold onto negative emotions, grudges, or regrets that weigh us down. These emotional burdens can prevent us from experiencing joy in the present moment. Learning to forgive others—and ourselves—can be incredibly freeing. Letting go of past hurt allows us to move forward with a lighter heart, making room for happiness to enter our lives.

The pursuit of happiness is a lifelong journey, one that requires patience, self-awareness, and a willingness to grow. It's important to remember that happiness is not a destination but a process. We will have moments of joy and moments of struggle, but through it all, we can find meaning and fulfillment by focusing on the things that truly matter—our relationships, our values, and our personal growth.

In the end, happiness is about living a life that feels authentic to us, where we embrace both the highs and lows with grace and acceptance. It's about taking the time to appreciate the small moments, finding gratitude in the present, and focusing on what we can control. By cultivating inner peace, fostering meaningful relationships, and aligning our actions with our values, we can create a life that is rich in happiness, no matter the circumstances.

RELATIONSHIP:

When talking about relationships, let's start with family relationships such as mom, dad, brother, and sister. Some of us are born with a loving and supporting family, which is great. However, some are born in families that are not so caring. We must deal with it; love it, or hate it, their blood runs through you, too. I remember when I was twelve, I felt suffocation toward my own family, not that I didn't love them, but I just felt the need to get away (probably due to growing up). I was fortunate to have an understanding mom, so at the tender age of fourteen, I left home and went to the United States of America to finish high school. Again, the family loves them or hates them. Love a relationship with someone; some get lucky and find that elusive true love, and be happy for them, but for others, it's not so great; but it's okay. You can find another one, a girlfriend/boyfriend, a spouse, not unlike the family you are born with. Looking for a great partner in life is a hit or miss affair sometimes, so just be patient when getting into a serious relationship because it can be time-consuming and a financial disaster waiting to happen (not to mention fatal). When it comes to relationships with friends, all I can say is, "time will tell." Some friends are only around when they need you, or something from you; a friend to me is always there when you feel down or are in trouble. I believe that the foundation of a relationship should be respected; on top of loving one another, there should be respect; we may agree or disagree with each other, may not be aligned with each other's views in life, but we must respect one another to move on. Anger must not be the outcome of a disagreement between friends.

Relationships are a cornerstone of human existence. They shape who we are and influence how we experience life. From family ties to friendships and romantic connections, relationships can bring both joy and challenges. Let's explore the complexities of relationships and what makes them meaningful.

Family Relationships

Family relationships are the first connections we form in life. Whether we have a close-knit, supportive family or one that is more distant or complicated, family bonds often play a significant role in shaping our identity. From the moment we are born, we are surrounded by family members who influence us in various ways. Parents, siblings, and extended family all contribute to our understanding of the world and our place in it.

For some, family is a source of unconditional love and support. They feel fortunate to be part of a family that is there for them through thick and thin. These family members celebrate each other's successes, offer help during tough times, and provide a safe space for one another. In this kind of family, love is often freely given, and the relationship feels stable and comforting.

However, not everyone is blessed with a family like this. Some people struggle with toxic family dynamics, where love may be conditional or even absent. Family conflicts, emotional neglect, and misunderstandings can make relationships within the family difficult to navigate. Growing up in a challenging family environment can create emotional scars that take time to heal. For those who feel suffocated or misunderstood by their family, it can be difficult to find a sense of belonging.

Yet, family relationships—no matter how strained—remain important. Blood ties bind us together, and even if we can't always control the dynamics, we can still learn to manage them. In some cases, stepping away from the family environment for a period of time can provide the necessary space to grow and heal. For example, leaving home to study abroad or pursuing personal goals can give us a new perspective on family and help us navigate those relationships with more clarity and maturity.

Romantic Relationships

Romantic relationships are perhaps the most complicated and intricate type of relationship we experience. These relationships often come with high expectations and deep emotional investments. They can be the most fulfilling and the most painful at the same time. For many, the idea of finding "true love" is a lifelong pursuit. People search for someone who will understand them, share their values, and build a life together. It's an exciting journey, but it can also be filled with uncertainty.

Finding a romantic partner who is compatible can feel like a lottery. It's not always a straightforward process, and many people experience heartbreak and disappointment before finding someone they truly connect with. There's no magic formula for finding the perfect partner, and sometimes, it takes trial and error. Relationships require effort, communication, and patience. The early stages of love may be thrilling, but the real test comes when the honeymoon phase fades, and the couple faces challenges together.

It's important to recognize that not every romantic relationship is meant to last. Sometimes, we meet people who teach us valuable lessons about ourselves, even if the relationship doesn't endure. We may realize what we want and don't want in a partner, and these experiences help shape our future relationships. The key is to approach love with an open heart and to understand that not every relationship will work out, but each one contributes to our personal growth.

Even when you find a lasting partner, relationships require constant nurturing. Love is not a passive feeling but an active choice. It involves compromise, empathy, and an ongoing effort to understand each other's needs and desires. A healthy romantic relationship is built on mutual respect and trust. It's not about perfection, but about working through challenges together while remaining committed to each other's happiness.

Friendships

Friendships are another vital aspect of human connection. Unlike family, we choose our friends, and these relationships can be some of the most rewarding. A true friend is someone who supports you through good times and bad, someone who listens without judgment and offers advice when needed. Friendships provide an outlet for social connection and emotional expression. These relationships can offer the comfort of being yourself without the pressures of family or romantic obligations.

However, friendships can also be fickle. Not every friend will stand the test of time, and some may only be around when they need something from you. Friendships can evolve, and people change over time. Some friends may drift away, while others may become lifelong companions. The key to sustaining strong friendships is mutual effort and respect. It's important to invest time and energy into maintaining connections with friends who lift you up and bring positivity into your life.

Trust and honesty are the foundation of any good friendship. Without trust, it's difficult to build a meaningful relationship. Similarly, respect is a critical element. While friends may disagree on certain topics or have different viewpoints, mutual respect ensures that these differences don't undermine the bond. It's important to understand that not every friendship will be perfect, but the best friends are the ones who accept you as you are and support you through thick and thin.

A good friend doesn't just stand by your side during happy moments; they are there for you when life gets tough. They offer a shoulder to cry on, lend a helping hand, and remind you of your worth when you feel down. Friendships that stand the test of time are often based on shared experiences and the willingness to be there for each other no matter what.

The Role of Respect in Relationships

One of the most important ingredients for any relationship to thrive is respect. Respect is the foundation upon which all healthy relationships are built, whether with family, friends, or romantic partners. Without respect, relationships can become toxic, and conflicts can escalate. Respect involves acknowledging the other person's feelings, opinions, and boundaries, and treating them with kindness and consideration.

Respect also means being able to disagree without letting it damage the relationship. It's natural for people to have different viewpoints and perspectives, but it's essential to communicate those differences in a respectful way. In any relationship, there will be disagreements, but it's how we handle them that defines the relationship. Arguments can arise, but respect ensures that they are resolved constructively and not with anger or resentment.

For example, in a family dynamic, respecting each person's individuality is crucial. Each family member has their own personality, desires, and challenges, and understanding and honoring those differences can create a more harmonious environment. Similarly, in romantic relationships, respecting each other's space, needs, and goals strengthens the bond and fosters a sense of trust and security.

The Challenge of Navigating Difficult Relationships

Not all relationships are easy. Some relationships require constant work, especially when there are unresolved conflicts or difficult personalities involved. There are times when we find ourselves in toxic or unhealthy relationships that drain our energy and well-being. In such cases, it's important to set boundaries and make difficult decisions for the sake of our mental and emotional health.

Setting boundaries is an act of self-respect. It involves knowing what is acceptable behavior and what isn't, and communicating those boundaries to others. It's okay to say no when something doesn't feel right or when a relationship becomes too emotionally demanding. Respecting your own needs is not selfish; it's necessary for maintaining a healthy relationship with yourself and others.

In some cases, it may be necessary to distance ourselves from relationships that are detrimental to our well-being. While this can be painful, sometimes it's the best course of action to protect ourselves from further harm. Walking away from toxic relationships can open up space for healthier connections to grow.

Relationships are an essential part of life. They shape our experiences, influence our emotions, and help us navigate the complexities of the world. Family, romantic partners, and friends each contribute to our sense of connection and belonging. While relationships can bring immense joy, they also require effort, communication, and respect.

Building and maintaining healthy relationships takes time, but the rewards are immeasurable. A strong relationship—whether with family, friends, or a romantic partner—provides emotional support, personal growth, and a sense of fulfillment. By respecting one another, being patient, and understanding the value of both love and compromise, we can cultivate relationships that enrich our lives and make the world a better place.

Relationships are complex and multifaceted. They shape our lives in ways that we often don't even fully realize. Whether they are familial, romantic, or platonic, every relationship adds something to our journey. These bonds contribute to our sense of identity and well-being, and how we navigate them determines the quality of our interactions with the world. But relationships aren't always easy. They require effort, understanding, and a willingness to grow both as an individual and as part of a larger unit. Let's dive deeper into the nature of relationships and explore the impact they have on our lives.

Emotional Growth Through Relationships

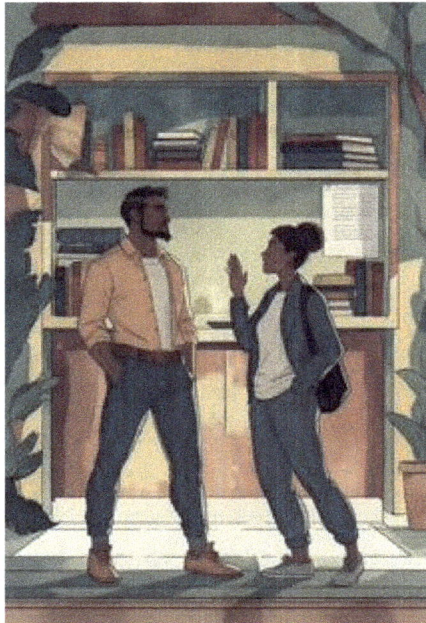

At the heart of every relationship is emotional growth. Relationships have a unique way of bringing out the best and sometimes the worst in us. They challenge us, push us, and force us to face parts of ourselves that we might not have been aware of. This growth can be beautiful, but it also comes with difficulties. When we are close to someone—whether it's a partner, family member, or friend—we often discover new things about ourselves that we might not have otherwise. Sometimes these realizations are uncomfortable, but they are essential for personal development.

For instance, in a romantic relationship, we may learn to compromise, share, and put the needs of someone else above our own. But we also learn about our own vulnerabilities and fears, such as insecurities, jealousy, or the fear of abandonment. These emotions, though challenging, provide an opportunity for deep self-reflection. Over time, with the right mindset, we can use these insights to grow into more empathetic and understanding individuals. In a way, relationships hold up a mirror, reflecting our emotions and behaviors, offering us a chance to adjust and become better versions of ourselves.

Family relationships also provide a unique form of emotional growth. The connection between parents and children, for example, is often a learning experience for both parties. Parents teach their children how to navigate life, but children also teach their parents about patience, resilience, and unconditional love. The roles may reverse over time, with parents relying on their children as they age. This cyclical nature of family relationships is a source of emotional depth that can be both grounding and transformative.

In friendships, emotional growth can be even more pronounced. Friendships often present us with opportunities to learn new perspectives. A good friend will listen to us, challenge us, and offer feedback that helps us see things in a new light. The best friendships are those that encourage us to be better, to strive for more, and to remain grounded in who we are. It's a give-and-take relationship that promotes both personal and shared growth.

The Importance of Communication

One of the most important elements of any relationship is communication. The way we communicate shapes our relationships and determines their success. Effective communication involves not only speaking honestly but also listening attentively. Many misunderstandings arise from poor communication, where people either fail to express themselves properly or don't listen with the intent to understand.

In romantic relationships, communication is essential. Often, issues arise because one partner feels unheard or misunderstood. Clear, open conversations can prevent small issues from escalating into larger problems. It's important to speak from the heart, but equally important to create an environment where the other person feels safe and comfortable expressing their feelings. This applies not just to intimate relationships but also to family relationships and friendships. When there is an open dialogue, people feel valued and respected, which strengthens the bond.

Listening is just as critical as speaking. Sometimes, all a person needs is to be heard, not necessarily fixed. When we listen attentively, we show that we care, that we are invested in the relationship and the other person's well-being. Too often, people focus on formulating their response rather than truly listening. But by focusing on the other person's words and feelings, we create space for genuine connection. Communication is a two-way street—one that requires effort, empathy, and mutual respect.

In family relationships, communication often takes on a more nurturing form. Parents must communicate with their children, guiding them and helping them understand the world. In turn, children communicate their feelings and needs to their parents, which helps build trust and understanding. As children grow older, this dynamic can shift, with parents learning to communicate more openly with their adult children. The importance of listening and expressing love and concern cannot be overstated, as these are the cornerstones of strong family ties.

Boundaries in Relationships

Another crucial aspect of healthy relationships is setting boundaries. Boundaries are necessary for maintaining individual identity and protecting one's emotional well-being. In any relationship, whether familial, romantic, or platonic, it's important to establish what is and isn't acceptable behavior. Boundaries create a sense of safety and respect, allowing people to feel secure and valued.

In romantic relationships, setting boundaries is vital to maintaining mutual respect and understanding. Each partner has their own needs, desires, and limits. Some may require more personal space, while others may feel more comfortable being in close proximity. These differences can lead to friction if not addressed openly. By having honest discussions about personal boundaries, partners can avoid misunderstandings and ensure that both individuals feel comfortable and respected.

Family dynamics also require boundaries, especially as children grow into adults. Parents must learn to respect their children's independence, while adult children must find ways to balance the expectations of their parents with their own lives. Healthy boundaries in family relationships prevent codependency and foster mutual respect. When everyone understands and respects each other's limits, the family can function as a cohesive unit without stifling anyone's personal growth.

Friendships, too, benefit from healthy boundaries. While friends should be there for each other, it's important that both individuals maintain their independence and don't rely on one another for constant emotional support. Boundaries help preserve the integrity of the relationship, ensuring that it remains balanced and fulfilling.

The Role of Trust in Relationships

Trust is the foundation upon which all strong relationships are built. Without trust, relationships can quickly deteriorate. Trust allows us to be vulnerable, knowing that the other person will not betray us. It creates a safe space for emotional intimacy and personal connection. Without trust, individuals in relationships are likely to experience anxiety, fear, and doubt, which can ultimately erode the bond.

In romantic relationships, trust is paramount. Partners need to trust each other not only with their hearts but also with their dreams, their fears, and their vulnerabilities. When trust is broken, it can take a long time to rebuild, and even then, the relationship may never be the same. It's important to establish trust early on and maintain it through honesty, integrity, and consistency. This can be difficult at times, especially when faced with challenges, but it's essential to creating a strong, lasting partnership.

Trust in family relationships is equally important. Parents must trust their children to make good decisions, and children must trust that their parents have their best interests at heart. When trust is broken in a family, it can have lasting emotional consequences. Similarly, in friendships, trust allows for deeper connections and understanding. When a friend shares something personal, they trust that their confidence will be respected. Trust nurtures loyalty and solidifies the bond between friends.

Handling Conflict

Conflict is an inevitable part of any relationship. No two people will always agree on everything, and differences of opinion or personality clashes can arise. However, it's how we handle conflict that determines the future of a relationship. Healthy conflict resolution involves being able to disagree respectfully, listen to the other person's point of view, and find common ground.

In romantic relationships, conflict can stem from miscommunication, unmet needs, or outside pressures. It's important to approach conflict with a calm and open mindset, focusing on finding solutions rather than assigning blame. Avoiding escalation is key, as harsh words or actions can cause irreparable damage. Instead of focusing on winning the argument, partners should aim for compromise and mutual understanding.

Family relationships can also involve conflict, especially during times of stress or change. Parents and children may disagree on lifestyle choices, or siblings may argue over family matters. The key is to maintain respect for one another's perspectives and find ways to resolve differences without letting them create long-lasting resentment.

Friendships are not immune to conflict either. Disagreements between friends are natural, but it's important to address them quickly and openly. Sometimes, it's necessary to apologize or offer an explanation to preserve the friendship. Open and honest communication is the best way to navigate conflict and keep relationships strong.

From family to romantic partners to friends, each relationship plays a role in our personal growth and happiness. At their best, relationships offer love, support, and a sense of belonging. But they also require effort, patience, and understanding. Communication, trust, boundaries, and conflict resolution are all essential to maintaining healthy relationships. It's through these connections that we experience life's fullest meaning and potential, growing together as we navigate the highs and lows of our journey.

SCHOOL:

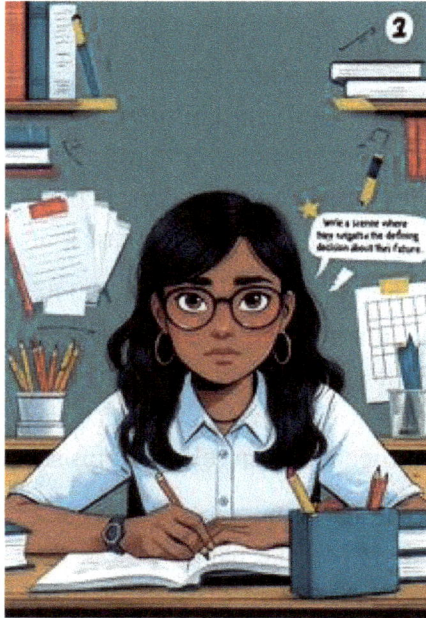

School establishments are not the only place you can get your education; for me, school means a place of learning, but school is not the only place you can get your education; there Are now multiple avenues where you can get your education, certificate, or diploma. Back then, before the internet age, you get your education from school establishment, vocational, and mentorship. Nowadays, you get all of that, plus you can get your education online, depending on where you want to be financially and professionally. If you want to be rich financially, you don't have to have a certificate or diploma, but you do need to have at least a high school diploma; though you don't have to, it does help along the way. You don't have to have a certificate or diploma to be rich. Through mentorship in the trade you wish to be in, you can achieve financial freedom, and with personal experiences learned from the do's and don'ts of business, you can achieve wealth as well. With so much information you can get from the internet, you can get educated by researching and exploring the vast knowledge it gives. Taking notes from other people's experiences and their commentary on how they achieved their goals is a piece of priceless advice and learning that you can apply to yourself. If you want to be a professional, such as a doctor, engineer, or lawyer, you need a diploma because it is required, and this field of work requires a specialized type of learning. Suppose you are talented, such as a singer, actor/actress, or athlete. In that case, this is a big money business where you can earn a lot of money and be rich, but be mindful of how you use your money, invest it wisely because, like a singer and actor/actress, you only make money when there is work to be done. If you are an athlete, you are only as good if you are physically able.

School has traditionally been the primary avenue for education, a place where students gather to learn from teachers and gain the knowledge needed to succeed in life. However, education is not confined to a classroom or a school building. Today, the concept of education has expanded, and there are multiple pathways to learning, each catering to different needs, goals, and circumstances. From online courses to mentorships, the opportunities to learn have multiplied, making education more accessible than ever before.

In the past, obtaining an education was relatively straightforward. The primary means were formal schooling, vocational training, and apprenticeship programs. If you wanted to learn a trade, you might have entered a vocational school or become an apprentice under the guidance of someone experienced in the field. If you sought higher learning, a university degree was often the ticket to advancement. These paths are still valid and important today, but the ways we approach education have evolved dramatically, especially with the advent of the internet.

The internet has transformed education by opening up an entire world of knowledge. You no longer have to be physically present in a classroom to receive an education. Today, you can take courses from prestigious institutions, learn new skills, or even earn a certificate or degree from the comfort of your home. Websites like Coursera, edX, and Udemy provide access to courses in a vast array of subjects—from business to technology to the arts. The flexibility of online learning allows individuals to balance their education with work, family, or other commitments. This means that more people can access higher education than ever before, especially those who may have previously been unable to attend traditional schools due to geographic or financial limitations.

However, while the internet offers vast resources, the traditional education system still holds importance in certain fields. Professions such as medicine, law, and engineering require highly specialized knowledge that typically can only be acquired through formal schooling and certification. These fields have stringent educational requirements because the stakes are high. A mistake made by a doctor or a lawyer can have serious consequences, so it's essential that professionals in these areas undergo rigorous training and testing to ensure they are prepared for the responsibilities of their careers. In these cases, a diploma or degree is not just a piece of paper; it represents years of focused study, hands-on experience, and the acquisition of specific skills necessary to perform critical tasks in society.

On the other hand, when it comes to achieving financial success, education in the traditional sense may not always be required. In many cases, financial freedom and wealth can be achieved through other means, such as entrepreneurship or working in skilled trades. The stories of many successful entrepreneurs reveal that, while education certainly helps, it is not always necessary for achieving great wealth. People like Steve Jobs, Bill Gates, and Richard Branson, who are among the wealthiest individuals in the world, did not complete their formal education in the traditional sense, yet they achieved remarkable success in business.

The key to success in many of these cases was mentorship and hands-on experience. Learning directly from those who have been successful in a particular field can be invaluable. In some professions, particularly in trades like carpentry, plumbing, or electrical work, apprenticeships and mentorships remain an important way to gain the necessary skills. These experiences provide practical, on-the-job learning that is often more useful than classroom instruction. Through mentorship, you can learn the ins and outs of a business or trade, gaining wisdom and guidance from someone who has already navigated the challenges you're likely to face. This type of education—based on real-world experience—can be just as valuable, if not more so, than a degree from a university.

That being said, there are still challenges in the pursuit of financial success without formal education. While it is possible to build wealth without a degree, it is important to acknowledge that this path requires a lot of hard work, perseverance, and sometimes a bit of luck. There is a level of risk involved in entrepreneurship or pursuing a career without a formal qualification. Without the safety net that a traditional education might provide, you need to have a strong understanding of business, financial management, and personal discipline. Those who succeed without degrees often possess a strong entrepreneurial spirit, a willingness to learn, and the ability to adapt to new opportunities.

For those who choose non-traditional career paths, such as artists, athletes, or entertainers, the formula for success looks different. While these fields can be highly lucrative, they also come with their own set of challenges. Talent and skill are certainly important in these industries, but so is timing, marketing, and luck. In addition, many of these professions are unstable—an athlete's career can be cut short by injury, and an actor or musician may face years of obscurity before they finally hit it big. It is crucial to be financially responsible in these industries, as the money can come quickly but may also disappear just as fast. Managing income wisely, investing in long-term opportunities, and planning for the future are essential for those who achieve success in these fields.

As a result, it is important to recognize that while education in the traditional sense may not be necessary to build wealth or success, it is still crucial to be well-informed. In any field, having a deep understanding of the industry you are involved in is key to long-term sustainability. This is where self-education, research, and continuous learning come into play. Even for those who do not pursue formal education, there is still an enormous wealth of knowledge available to help guide you through your career.

Self-learning, whether through books, online resources, or mentorship, has become an integral part of personal and professional growth. It is no longer enough to just rely on what you learn in school; successful people are often those who continue to educate themselves throughout their lives. Whether it's gaining a deeper understanding of a specific field, improving interpersonal skills, or staying up to date on industry trends, ongoing education is essential. The internet offers unlimited resources to facilitate this kind of learning, and platforms like YouTube and podcasts can be incredibly valuable for acquiring new knowledge and insights.

The wealth of information available online also allows for more specialized forms of education. If you're interested in a niche topic—whether it's coding, digital marketing, graphic design, or something else entirely—there are courses and communities dedicated to that subject matter. Online learning enables people to pursue their passions and develop specialized skills that might not be covered in a traditional classroom setting.

Education today is no longer a one-size-fits-all model. Whether you choose the traditional route of attending school or decide to take a more unconventional approach through mentorship or self-learning, there are countless ways to gain the knowledge and skills needed for success. In the end, it's not just about obtaining a diploma or certificate—it's about continuously striving to learn and grow, adapting to new opportunities, and remaining open to the many paths that can lead to personal and professional fulfillment. As we navigate the changing landscape of education, one thing is clear: the power to shape your future is in your hands, and learning is a lifelong journey.

HATERS:

Let people judge you.

Let them misunderstand you.

Let them gossip about you.

What they think of you isn't your problem.

Their opinions do not pay your bills.

So, you stay kind, committed to love,

And no matter what they do or say…

Never doubt your worth or the beauty of your worth.

You keep shining and let the haters hate.

PESSIMIST VS OPTIMIST:

Which one are you? First, let us define them. A Pessimist is a person who tends to see the worst aspect of things or believe that the worst will happen. A person who thinks this world is as bad as it could be or that evil will ultimately prevail over good. In contrast, an optimist is a person who tends to be hopeful and confident about the future or the success of something. A person who believes that this world is the best of all possible worlds or that good must ultimately prevail over evil.

I believe that people are born with this type of character or influenced by their surroundings, and I think there is nothing wrong with being a pessimist. However, it is a negative way of thinking, and I also believe that we need to have both, like yen and yang, night and day, good vs. evil; though it is different from One another, we need to find the balance to co-exist.

Growing up, I was a pessimist; I had this negative mentality. However, when I got married and started my own family, I was even more damaged in life because of financial issues and marital issues that almost cost me my marriage. So, one day, I was overwhelmed with all of life's problems, my back against the wall. I just surrendered my life to the lord. I never was a religious person, but ever since that day, I have been praying every day, whenever I am driving to work in the comfort of my car and saying thank you, lord, for all the blessings that you have given me and everything that you will be given me in the future (I affirm this to the lord), just being grateful for everything. Significant or minor problems don't worry me because I believe in the lord; he will always be there for me. It reminds Me of the phrase "footprint in the sand." So NO, if you are thinking that my life is any better now than what my life was before, it's just now I know how to deal with my problems much better. Switching my pessimistic mentality to an optimistic mentality Is life-changing. Remember what I said earlier about the yen and the yang, the night and day? I have walked in the darkness before, but now I have switched on the light and can see much better, from night into day.

Which One Are You?

Have you ever paused to wonder which lens you view the world through? Are you someone who sees challenges as insurmountable obstacles or as opportunities for growth? This difference lies at the heart of being either a pessimist or an optimist.

Let's start by defining these terms. A **pessimist** is someone who tends to focus on the negative side of situations, often anticipating the worst possible outcome. They may feel that the world is inherently flawed, that life's challenges are overwhelming, and that misfortune is unavoidable. For pessimists, the glass is perpetually half-empty, and they believe that evil or hardship will ultimately triumph over good.

On the other hand, an **optimist** approaches life with hope and confidence. They are resilient, often finding silver linings even in the darkest of clouds. For optimists, the glass is not only half-full but brimming with possibilities. They trust in the idea that, despite setbacks, good will ultimately prevails over evil, and life offers more blessings than curses.

Nature, Nurture, and the Balance Between

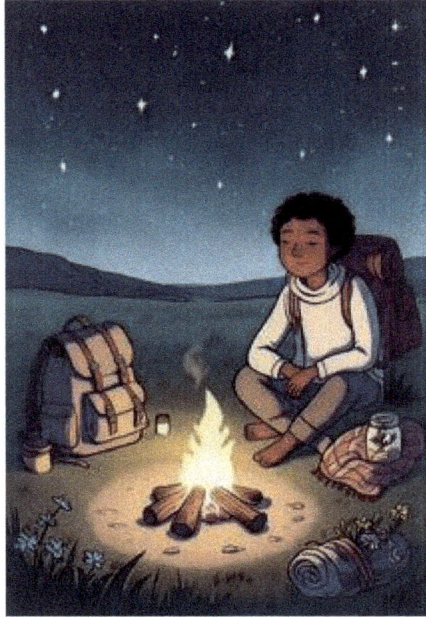

I believe our tendency toward pessimism or optimism is shaped by both our innate nature and the influence of our surroundings. Some people may be born with a predisposition toward one mindset, while others develop their outlook based on their life experiences. For instance, growing up in an environment filled with encouragement, love, and positivity can nurture an optimistic perspective. Conversely, prolonged exposure to hardships or negativity may foster a more pessimistic outlook.

There's nothing inherently wrong with being either a pessimist or an optimist. Like **yin and yang**, night and day, or good and evil, both mindsets serve a purpose in our lives. Pessimism, while often perceived as "negative," can actually help us prepare for challenges, mitigate risks, and make practical decisions. Optimism, on the other hand, inspires hope, resilience, and innovation. The key is not to lean too heavily on one side but to find balance—a harmony that allows us to co-exist with both perspectives.

My Journey: From Darkness to Light

I once heard a story about a man wishing to die because as he felt no one cared about him. When asked if he had a family, he replied "yes". When asked if they took care and spoke to him, he again answered "yes". Finally, when asked if he lived in a community where people greeted him with "hi" or "hello," again he replied "yes." Then, the questioner said, "There you go, there are people who care about you more than you thought."

Some people stop living fully because they believe no one cares about them. But as humans, we are inherently capable of caring, loving, hating, and feeling sadness—no one can deny that. On your final day, what will your last thoughts be? Perhaps you'll wonder: Did I do my best with this life?

Have I achieved what I set out to do? Have I been good or bad? Am I living a better life than when I started? Are my loved ones prepared for my absence? Will I go to heaven or hell? This last question often lingers as life ends, and the answer depends on how we've lived. If I've neither harmed nor helped, do I deserve heaven? If I've done nothing to make the world better, can I expect a reward?

We should always strive to do good—improving ourselves, helping others, and caring for nature and animals. Every new day is a chance to live with purpose and kindness.

QUOTE: STOP FEELING SORRY FOR YOURSELF, GET YOUR ASS UP, AND START WORKING.

The Power of Optimism

Shifting from a pessimistic to an optimistic mindset was like flipping a switch in a dark room. Suddenly, I could see clearly. The problems that once seemed insurmountable were now manageable. Instead of being paralyzed by fear, I took action with confidence, trusting that even setbacks were part of a larger plan.

This doesn't mean that life is perfect. I still face difficulties, but I no longer let them define me. Optimism doesn't erase hardships—it equips you to handle them with grace and perseverance.

One of the most powerful lessons I've learned is that optimism is a choice. While circumstances might push us toward negativity, we have the power to reframe our perspective. By focusing on solutions rather than problems, on blessings rather than burdens, we can transform our outlook and, ultimately, our lives.

Balancing Light and Darkness

As I reflect on my journey, I've come to appreciate the value of both pessimism and optimism. Pessimism taught me caution and preparedness. It made me a realist, someone who acknowledges the difficulties of life and takes steps to address them. But it was optimism that gave me the courage to rise above those difficulties, to believe in a brighter future, and to take risks for the sake of growth and happiness.

Life is a delicate dance between light and darkness, between struggle and triumph. Just as night gives way to day, our lives are a series of cycles—moments of hardship followed by moments of joy. The key is not to get stuck in one phase but to move through them with grace, learning and growing along the way.

Acknowledge your feelings. Whether you're naturally pessimistic or optimistic, honor your emotions without judgment. Accept where you are as the starting point for growth.

Practice gratitude. Gratitude is the cornerstone of optimism. By focusing on what you have rather than what you lack, you can shift your mindset and invite more positivity into your life.

Seek perspective. When facing challenges, try to see the bigger picture. Ask yourself: "What can I learn from this? How can this situation help me grow?"

Surround yourself with positivity. The people you spend time with greatly influence your mindset. Seek out individuals who uplift, inspire, and encourage you.

Embrace faith or purpose. Whether it's faith in God, a higher power, or simply in your own ability to overcome, having a sense of purpose can provide strength during difficult times.

Life will always have its ups and downs, its moments of light and darkness. But it's how we navigate those moments that defines us. Switching from a pessimistic to an optimistic mindset has been life-changing for me. It hasn't erased my struggles, but it has given me the tools to face them with courage, resilience, and hope.

To anyone feeling stuck in negativity, I want to remind you: you have the power to change. It starts with a simple decision to see the world differently. Like yin and yang, night and day, pessimism and optimism are two sides of the same coin. By finding balance, you can create a life filled with both realism and hope, challenges and triumphs, darkness and light.

AWAKENING:

I hope this book serves as an awakening for those who read this and for a better you. Please don't let the near-death experience come and tell yourself that "now I will change." don't let the new year be a signal for a new change because if you want to change, just do it, and keep doing it until your old habits are has been replaced with a good one. There is no better time to change than now. Don't hesitate to tell yourself, "I will do it next week or month." If there are changes that need to be made, do it. It may be hard at first, but eventually, you will change. Personally, if I had not changed from my old ways, such as eating and drinking habits, I would probably have had a stroke by now or worse, death; my body was sending me all these signals to change my eating habits that could lead to obesity, thank god that I did, because now I'm enjoying my life with my family, I am healthy, I'm not into any medication (knock on wood I would never have to) awakening your mind to a positive mindset will give you a positive outlook into life. If you keep watching or listening to negative people or harmful content on television shows, guess what? You will get a negative perspective in life; it is no secret that when bad things influence you, your actions tend to be negative. Experiment: try watching funny shows sometimes that will make you laugh or watch cut cats or dogs or babies; you will feel better afterward; watch the world's beauty, listen to motivational speakers or inspirational speakers, and you will be like, "What am I listening to?" Because you are not used to it, feel that discomfort in your ears or body because it is out of your norms, that is why you have to get out of your comfort zone, be awakened from your extended old self, and be a new you. That you thought you could never achieve.

I hope that it will inspire you to take control of your life, not tomorrow, not next week, but today. Waiting for the "perfect moment" to change is one of the biggest traps we fall into. There is no such thing as a perfect moment—only the moment you decide to act. Don't let a brush with death, a frightening health scare, or a major personal loss be the reason you finally decide to change. These moments can be transformative, yes, but why wait for pain or regret to drive you? Instead, act now.

Change isn't always easy, but it is always possible. It's like planting a seed: at first, you don't see the growth, and the work feels endless. You're watering and waiting, and the soil looks the same day after day. But if you stay consistent, the seed will eventually sprout. The same is true of change. The hard part is trusting the process when you don't see results right away. This is where most people give up. They lose faith because they expect immediate rewards. Don't fall into that trap. Growth is happening even when it's invisible.

When I look back at my own life, I see how crucial it was for me to wake up and realize that my old ways were leading me down a dangerous path. My eating habits were terrible. I ignored my health, indulged in junk food, and let stress dictate my choices. At the time, it felt normal—I wasn't doing anything drastically different from what others around me were doing. But my body was sending me warning signals: fatigue, weight gain, constant aches, and a sense of sluggishness that I couldn't shake. I brushed it off until one day, I realized I was gambling with my future. If I hadn't made the decision to change, I might not be here today.

Making that shift wasn't easy. It required me to take a hard look at my habits, my mindset, and the excuses I had been telling myself for years. The first step was acknowledging that my life wouldn't improve unless I took responsibility for it. No one else could save me—not my family, not my friends, and certainly not my past self. The only person who could make a difference was me.

Therefore, I started small. I didn't overhaul my entire life in one day— that would've been overwhelming and unsustainable. Instead, I focused on one change at a time. I swapped out unhealthy snacks for fruits and vegetables. I started walking for just 15 minutes a day, which gradually turned into 30 minutes, then an hour. I replaced sugary drinks with water. These small steps added up, and over time, they became habits.

But it wasn't just about physical health. Awakening is as much a mental and emotional journey as it is a physical one. I realized that my thoughts were often my biggest enemy. I had a tendency to dwell on negativity, to replay old mistakes, and to worry about things that hadn't even happened yet. This pessimistic mindset was holding me back more than I realized.

Changing my thoughts was harder than changing my diet or exercise routine. Our minds are incredibly stubborn—they cling to familiar patterns, even if those patterns are harmful. To break free, I had to become more intentional about what I allowed into my mind. I stopped consuming content that made me feel anxious or angry. I limited my exposure to negative news and toxic social media. Instead, I filled my mind with positivity: uplifting books, motivational speeches, and inspiring stories of people who had overcome challenges.

One of the most powerful tools I discovered was gratitude. Every morning, I started writing down three things I was grateful for. At first, it felt forced. I struggled to come up with even one thing some days. But over time, it became a habit, and I noticed a shift in my perspective. Instead of focusing on what I didn't have or what was going wrong, I began to appreciate the good things in my life—even the small things, like a sunny day or a kind word from a stranger. Gratitude rewired my brain to see the world through a more positive lens.

Another key part of my awakening was learning to embrace discomfort. Growth rarely happens in our comfort zones. The habits that feel easy and familiar are often the ones that keep us stuck. To change, you have to be willing to challenge yourself. This might mean waking up earlier, saying no to unhealthy temptations, or stepping into situations that make you nervous. Discomfort is a sign that you're growing—it's the price of transformation.

If you're reading this and thinking, "That sounds great, but I don't know where to start," here's my advice: start small, but start now. Pick one thing you want to change and take one step toward it today. It could be as simple as drinking a glass of water instead of soda or going for a short walk instead of scrolling on your phone. The action itself doesn't have to be big—it just has to be intentional.

And remember, change is not a straight line. You will have setbacks. There will be days when you fall back into old habits or feel like giving up. That's okay. What matters is that you don't let those moments define you. Each day is a new opportunity to try again. Progress isn't about perfection—it's about persistence.

As you embark on your journey, be patient with yourself. Change takes time, and the results are rarely immediate. But I promise you this: the effort is worth it. When you look back a year from now, you'll be amazed at how far you've come. The things that once seemed impossible will become second nature.

Awakening your mind, body, and spirit is the greatest gift you can give yourself. It's about reclaiming your power and realizing that you are not a victim of your circumstances. You have the ability to shape your life, no matter where you're starting from.

One final thought: never underestimate the impact your transformation can have on others. When you change for the better, you inspire those around you to do the same. Your positive energy becomes contagious, and you become a source of hope and motivation for your family, friends, and even strangers.

So, let today be the day you awaken. Not next week, not next month—now. Take that first step, no matter how small it may seem. Believe in yourself, trust the process, and remember that every great journey begins with a single step. Your future self will thank you.

FOOTPRINTS:

One night, a man had a dream. He dreamed he was walking along the beach with the lord. Across the sky, he flashed scenes from his life. For each scene, he noticed two sets of footprints in the sand; one belonged to him, and the other to the lord.

When the last scene of his life flashed before him, he looked back at the footprints in the sand; he noticed that many times along the path of his life, there was only one set of footprints. He also noticed that it happened at his lowest and saddest times.

This bothered him, and he questioned the lord about it.

"Lord, you said that once I followed you, you'd walk with me all the way. But I have noticed that during the most troublesome times in my life, there is only one set of footprints. I don't understand why, when I needed you the most, you would leave me."

The Lord replied, "My precious child, I love you, and I would never leave you during your times of trial and suffering. When you see only one set of footprints, it was then that I carried you.

FIGHTER:

All of us are fighters within our rights, but do you know what a real fighter looks like? He is the one that never gives up. The one that fights no matter the circumstances, you persevere and keep fighting despite all troubles and issues. Because for every problem, there is a solution. The most significant challenge we face in our lives is our self. A person fails because they give up. Those who succeed are the ones who fight; whenever we are met with a problem, we look no further for a solution because it is within us. Be humble and pray and ask for guidance from god. Remember, when you are down and out, you are not alone. God is always there with you and will guide you, but you must do everything possible to get out of your problems, work hard, and put in those hours to do whatever you want to achieve because hard work pays. Remember, you are a fighter. You have to show it.

Being a fighter means you learn to embrace struggle as an inevitable part of growth. Life is full of moments when it feels easier to surrender—to give in to despair, to let go of dreams, or to retreat from challenges. But what defines a fighter is their refusal to give up, no matter how daunting the battle may appear. Each fight, whether big or small, carves a path to resilience, shaping us into stronger, wiser, and more determined individuals.

One of the most formidable opponents you will ever face is yourself. The doubts, fears, and insecurities that creep into your mind can be more challenging to defeat than any external enemy. These inner battles often whisper lies: "You're not good enough," "You'll never make it," or "Why even try?" These voices can be loud and convincing, but a fighter knows that the strength to silence them lies within. Fighting yourself is about learning to replace negativity with hope, doubt with faith, and fear with courage. It is about standing tall even when the weight of the world feels too heavy to bear.

Consider the countless stories of individuals who have overcome monumental challenges. From those who have triumphed over physical disabilities to achieve greatness, to people who have risen from poverty to create lives of meaning and success, the common thread is perseverance. These individuals didn't succeed because life handed them an easy road; they succeeded because they chose to fight every single day.

Think of the single parent working multiple jobs to provide for their children, sacrificing their own comforts for the sake of their family's future. Or the student who spends sleepless nights studying to break free from generational hardship and build a better tomorrow. These are fighters, not because they never feel exhausted or discouraged, but because they keep going.

A fighter doesn't ignore their struggles; instead, they confront them head-on. There is no shame in feeling tired, afraid, or even defeated at times. What matters is that you don't let those feelings define you. To be a fighter is to rise after every fall, to learn from mistakes, and to face each new day with a renewed sense of determination.

One of the essential lessons a fighter learns is the importance of prayer and humility. Asking for guidance from God is not a sign of weakness but a profound act of strength. When we acknowledge that we cannot do it all on our own, we open ourselves to divine wisdom and support. Prayer doesn't necessarily change our circumstances overnight, but it changes *us*. It fortifies our spirit, reminds us of our purpose, and fills us with the faith needed to keep moving forward.

When you feel lost, remember that you are never truly alone. God walks with you, even in the darkest valleys. Often, it is in the most challenging moments that we feel His presence the strongest—when we are on our knees, broken and weary. He may not remove the obstacles in your path, but He gives you the strength to climb over them, the wisdom to navigate around them, or the courage to break through them.

But faith alone is not enough. A true fighter knows that action must accompany prayer. You cannot sit idly by, waiting for life to improve. It requires work—dedicated, relentless effort. Success is rarely handed to anyone; it is earned through perseverance, sweat, and sacrifice. Whether it's waking up earlier to pursue your goals, putting in extra hours at work, or making difficult choices to stay on the right path, your commitment to the fight is what will lead to victory.

Hard work is a testament to your fighting spirit. Every hour you pour into your dreams is a step closer to turning them into reality. There will be days when the progress feels slow, when it seems like all your effort is in vain. But remember, success is not about instant results—it is about consistency. Brick by brick, day by day, fighters build their future, even when the end goal feels distant.

It's also crucial to recognize that being a fighter doesn't mean going it alone. Fighters know when to seek help and lean on others for support. There is strength in community, in surrounding yourself with people who lift you up and encourage you to keep going. Whether it's family, friends, mentors, or faith leaders, these individuals remind you of your worth and potential, especially on days when you forget.

A fighter understands that every battle has a purpose. The struggles you face today are shaping you for something greater tomorrow. The pain, frustration, and setbacks are all part of a refining process, like fire molding steel. Each challenge you overcome adds to your strength, your resilience, and your character. It teaches you lessons that will prepare you for future battles, making you wiser and more capable.

Even when the outcome isn't what you hoped for, being a fighter means finding meaning in the fight itself. Success isn't always about winning; sometimes, it's about the courage to try, the growth that comes from the struggle, and the dignity of knowing you gave it your all.

There will be times when the fight feels endless, when you're tempted to throw in the towel. In those moments, remind yourself why you started. Think of the people counting on you, the dreams you hold dear, and the version of yourself you aspire to become. Draw strength from your purpose and let it fuel you to keep pushing forward.

As you journey through life, remember that fighting is not just about surviving—it's about thriving. It's about finding joy and meaning even in the midst of challenges. A fighter learns to celebrate small victories, to find gratitude in every step of progress, no matter how small. Gratitude transforms the fight from a burden into an opportunity, a chance to grow and become better.

Being a fighter is about embracing the belief that no matter how hard life gets, you have the strength to overcome. It is about knowing that within you lies the power to face anything life throws your way. You are capable of enduring, persevering, and ultimately triumphing—not because the road is easy, but because you refuse to give up.

So, stand tall. Wear your scars as badges of honor, proof that you have fought and survived. Let each battle you face remind you of the strength and resilience you possess. When the world tries to knock you down, stand firm in your faith, your determination, and your courage.

Remember: you are a fighter. You always have been. You always will be. Keep fighting, not just for the battles you face today but for the victories waiting for you tomorrow.

UNDER-PRESSURE:

We all react differently to pressure, but I'm one of those people who "the when going gets tough, the tough get going." person time seems to slow down on me when I'm under pressure; my mind shifts to focus on being scared or angry or confused, even hopelessness. Like I said, people react differently under pressure. Also, one of my secrets is prayer; I pray a lot. My life is full of challenges; I can't complain about my problems. I always compare my issues to others; my problems are nothing compared to them. And I am grateful for my life, and that is the thing too: always be thankful for what you have in life, and not the one you don't have; if you have something you feel you need, work hard for it.

Under-pressure is synonymous with anyone's problem, and just like any problem, we deal with it; problems don't just go away on their own; we deal with them, look for solutions, and eventually find the answer.

Never think that when you have a problem, it is something new and that this problem has never been dealt with before; your problem/issues are not something new; you may be new to this type of problem. If you don't know the answer to a problem, ask a family member, a friend, a co-worker, or better yet, a professional. We all get overwhelmed sometimes, but there is the answer to problems.

Pressure is a part of life that we all encounter in different forms and degrees. Some people face pressure in the form of tight deadlines at work, others in family responsibilities, health concerns, financial troubles, or even personal growth. Regardless of the source, pressure has a unique way of pushing us out of our comfort zones and testing our resilience. It doesn't discriminate—no one is immune to it. What sets us apart is how we respond when the weight of pressure bears down on us.

For me, pressure can be both a catalyst and a challenge. There are moments when it feels like I'm carrying the weight of the world on my shoulders. My thoughts race, emotions swell, and doubts creep in. Yet, through it all, I've learned that pressure has the power to refine us. Just as heat and pressure turn coal into diamonds, the challenges we face can mold us into stronger, more capable individuals if we persevere.

One of the most valuable lessons I've learned about dealing with pressure is the importance of staying present. It's easy to get overwhelmed when you're thinking about the what-ifs or focusing on the sheer size of the problem ahead. But breaking the situation into manageable steps has been a game-changer for me. Instead of viewing pressure as a mountain I have to conquer all at once, I've learned to see it as a series of small hills that I can climb one step at a time.

Prayer has been a cornerstone of my ability to handle pressure. When I feel like the walls are closing in, I take a moment to pray. It doesn't matter where I am—in the car, at home, or even in a crowded room. Prayer gives me clarity and a sense of calm amidst the chaos. It reminds me that I'm not alone in this journey, that there's a higher power guiding me, even when I don't have all the answers. There's a peace that comes with surrendering your burdens, knowing that while you may not have control over everything, you have faith in something greater.

Another powerful tool for managing pressure is gratitude. When we're under pressure, our focus often narrows to the problem at hand, making it easy to forget all the good things in our lives. But pausing to count your blessings can provide a sense of perspective. It doesn't mean your challenges disappear, but it helps to remind yourself of what you have, rather than what you lack. Gratitude is grounding; it anchors you to the positive aspects of your life, even in turbulent times.

Perspective is another critical aspect of handling pressure. No matter how overwhelming a problem feels, chances are, someone else has faced a similar situation—or worse—and has found a way through it. While comparing problems isn't meant to diminish your feelings, it can be a humbling reminder that struggles are universal. Sometimes, this perspective makes our burdens feel a little lighter and our ability to tackle them a little stronger.

I've also found that seeking help is an underrated but incredibly effective way to cope with pressure. We often think we have to solve everything on our own, but that's far from the truth. There's strength in admitting you need support and reaching out to those around you. Whether it's a trusted family member, a friend, a colleague, or a professional, leaning on others can provide fresh insights, comfort, and guidance. Often, the very act of talking through a problem can help you see solutions you hadn't considered before.

Pressure often reveals our inner resilience and resourcefulness. Think about a time when you were overwhelmed but managed to come out on the other side. At the moment, it may have felt impossible, but you made it through. Remembering those victories can serve as a reminder of your capability and give you confidence to face new challenges.

It's also important to recognize that pressure doesn't always have to be a negative force. Sometimes, it's the very thing that propels us toward growth and achievement. When you think about the greatest accomplishments in your life, chances are they weren't handed to you without effort. The pressure to succeed, to improve, or to overcome often pushes us to dig deeper and discover strengths we didn't know we had.

For instance, there have been times in my life when I felt overwhelmed by financial difficulties or personal setbacks. In those moments, the pressure seemed unbearable. But instead of letting it break me, I used it as fuel. I worked harder, sought advice, and stayed persistent. Looking back now, I realize that those tough moments shaped me into the person I am today.

One of the hardest things about pressure is that it often comes with uncertainty. We don't know how things will turn out, and that lack of control can be terrifying. But I've learned that worrying about the unknown only adds to the burden. Instead, I focus on what I can control—my actions, my mindset, and my effort. By shifting my focus to what's within my power, I regain a sense of agency, even in the face of uncertainty.

Another vital part of handling pressure is self-care. It might seem counterintuitive when you're under stress to take time for yourself, but it's essential. Whether it's going for a walk, meditating, journaling, or simply taking a few deep breaths, these small acts of self-care can make a significant difference. They give you a chance to reset, recharge, and approach your challenges with a clearer mind.

Physical health also plays a crucial role in managing pressure. When we're stressed, it's easy to neglect our bodies—skipping meals, losing sleep, or forgoing exercise. But these things only make it harder to cope. Taking care of your physical health—eating nutritious foods, staying active, and getting enough rest—can help you build the stamina and resilience needed to face challenges head-on.

In the end, pressure is an inevitable part of life. But how we respond to it is what defines us. Do we let it crush us, or do we use it as an opportunity to grow? It's not always easy, but every challenge we face is a chance to prove to ourselves that we're capable of more than we think.

When you're under pressure, remember this: you are stronger than you know. The very fact that you've faced difficulties before and are still here today is a testament to your resilience. So, take a deep breath, lean on your faith, seek support when needed, and keep moving forward. Pressure may test you, but it will never define you unless you let it.

Lastly, embrace the lessons that pressure teaches. Every challenge comes with an opportunity to learn—about yourself, about others, and about life. Sometimes, the lessons are hard, but they're always valuable. Pressure can reveal your weaknesses, but it can also illuminate your strengths. It can show you where you need to grow and what truly matters to you.

So, the next time you find yourself under pressure, see it not as a burden, but as a stepping stone. It's a chance to rise, to learn, and to become a better version of yourself. Because at the end of the day, it's not the absence of pressure that defines a successful life—it's the ability to face it with courage, grace, and perseverance.

HEARTACHE:

I envy those who have not experienced heartache. But not really, let me explain. In my teenage years, I had a big crush on a girl; back then, I was young, and I didn't know the difference between crushes and love; I thought they were the same. So I courted this girl and expressed my feelings to her. But being impatient just after the third attempt, I gave up and took that as a heartache; I felt devastated. This was the time I started drinking to drown my sorrows, and I had not drunk before this experience. Also, I believe this is the first time I courted a girl in my life and expressed my feelings, and I'm bum she didn't say yes, and she didn't say any either, but as I said, I was impatient. Fortunately, I have my family to support me; they talk to me and give me advice, and it helps.

When it's not meant to be, it's not meant to be. After that experience, I focused more on my studies in college and immersed myself in sports. I played basketball a lot at this time, and I also played martial arts tournaments. I can't remember how long I felt the heartache, but I guess maybe a few weeks and move on; I recover much faster, perhaps due to my heavy involvement in sports at this time and school work, and I thank my family support it helps a lot. That heartache did not stop me from looking for another girl to be my girlfriend; I had a few until I met my future wife.

The experience I learned from that heartache is that you really cannot and should not shed a single drop of tears in any person when that person does not have any feelings towards you. It is natural to be emotional or to have feelings for someone, but that emotion/feeling can trick you sometimes. Before we do anything emotional (predominantly negative), I suggest we step back, analyze/evaluate the situation, and ask ourselves if it's worth investing our time and emotion in that person. Remember…relationship is a two-way street, not one-way.

Heartache is an inevitable part that everyone faces at some point in life. It's the pain of loss, the sting of rejection, and the overwhelming sense of loneliness that can seem impossible to escape. But as I look back on that time when I was younger and feeling heartbroken, I realize how much it taught me. It wasn't just about the girl I liked or the feelings I had for her—it was about learning how to handle emotions, how to understand the significance of patience, and how to appreciate the support of those around you.

It's easy to romanticize the idea of love when you're young. You think that if someone doesn't return your feelings, then something must be wrong with you. But that's not true. Heartache taught me that love is not a transaction or a simple equation—it's a journey. It's about finding someone who complements your soul, someone who sees you for who you are, flaws and all. And it's just as much about timing as it is about compatibility. Sometimes, people come into your life for a season, and sometimes, they come to teach you a lesson. The girl I had a crush on wasn't the one I was meant to be with, and that's okay. The heartache didn't destroy me—it helped me grow.

In the aftermath of that initial heartbreak, I didn't know what to do with my feelings. They were foreign to me—so raw, so overwhelming. That's when I turned to distractions. I focused on my studies and immersed myself in sports. But it wasn't just the distraction itself that helped me—it was the mindset that came with it. Sports taught me to be resilient. It taught me how to push through pain, how to maintain focus even when everything felt chaotic around me. Every time I got a rebound in basketball, every time I threw a punch in martial arts, I learned that pain is temporary, but growth is constant.

It was during those days of intense physical exertion that I realized something vital: heartache, just like physical pain, is something that eventually fades away. No matter how intense the pain feels in the moment, it won't last forever. My focus shifted to what I could control—my own growth. By throwing myself into my passions and interests, I started to see that there was more to life than waiting for someone else to validate me or to make me feel complete. I had to find that validation within myself. I became my own source of strength, and that became one of the most powerful lessons I learned in my youth.

The support from my family also played a critical role during this period. They listened to me, they shared their wisdom, and they encouraged me to keep moving forward. At times, I thought they might be tired of hearing me talk about my broken heart, but they never showed it. Their unwavering support was like a lifeline, helping me keep my head above water when I felt like I was drowning in my own emotions. My family reminded me that it's okay to feel pain, but it's also important to allow yourself the space to heal.

That's another lesson I took from that experience: healing isn't linear. There were days when I felt like I had moved past the heartache, only to find myself back in the depths of sadness. The unpredictability of the emotional journey can be overwhelming. There's no straightforward path from pain to healing. But slowly, over time, the days of feeling lost became fewer and farther between. Each day, I found a little more peace, a little more clarity. Eventually, I no longer carried the weight of that heartache with me. It became a part of my past, something I could look back on and appreciate for the role it played in shaping me into the person I was becoming.

As I moved on and grew older, I had other relationships, some that ended in disappointment, others that didn't work out for reasons I couldn't control. Each one brought with it its own unique brand of heartache, but I was no longer the same person I was during that first experience. I had learned that heartache, while painful, wasn't something to fear—it was a part of the journey. Each breakup, each lost connection, taught me something new about myself. It taught me what I wanted in a relationship and what I needed to avoid. It helped me set boundaries, understand my worth, and know when to walk away from situations that no longer served me.

When I finally met my future wife, I was no longer the naive young person who thought that love could solve all problems. I had learned that love, while beautiful, is also a choice—a conscious decision to build something together, to support each other through thick and thin. Heartache had taught me that love wasn't about finding someone to complete me; it was about finding someone who complemented me, someone I could walk through life with, not just when things were good but also during the hardest times.

Even now, looking back at those early experiences, I realize how much they shaped my understanding of relationships and love. The heartache I once thought would destroy me became a teacher, imparting lessons that I still carry with me today. It helped me become more patient, more understanding, and more empathetic toward others. I now see heartache as a part of the human experience, something that connects us all. Whether it's the pain of unrequited love or the grief of losing someone close, we all experience heartache. But it doesn't have to define us. Instead, it can be the thing that propels us forward, that motivates us to become better versions of ourselves.

In the years that followed, I've come to realize that heartache is not just about romantic love—it applies to many different aspects of life. We experience heartache in our careers, when we fail to achieve our goals, when we lose our sense of purpose. We experience heartache when we lose a friend, when a chapter of our life ends, or when we face difficult challenges that seem insurmountable. Like romantic heartache, these other forms of heartache can be transformative. They test our resilience, they push us to dig deeper within ourselves, and they show us what we're truly capable of.

One of the most important during heartache is to be kind to ourselves. It's easy to get caught up in self-blame, to think that we're unworthy of love or success. But the truth is, everyone experiences heartache at some point, and it doesn't mean we're failures—it simply means we're human. I've had to remind myself that healing takes time, and that it's okay to be vulnerable and to ask for help when I need it. No one can do this life alone, and heartache is often a reminder of that.

Looking back, I don't envy those who have never experienced heartache. While it can be incredibly painful, it's also been one of the most important parts of my growth. It taught me to be resilient, to be patient, and to trust that everything in life has a purpose—even the painful moments. Heartache, in its own way, is a gift. It's a chance to learn, to grow, and to become stronger than we ever thought possible.

HOMELESSNESS:

I live here in the greatest country in the world and one of the wealthiest countries in the world, the United States of America, so there should be no reason that there are homeless people (men or women) living on the streets. Yet, homelessness is pretty much in major cities across the country. Please don't tell me that there are no jobs out there; there are jobs everywhere; people from different countries come here to work, and they would get one. So there is no reason a person cannot have a job here. There are so many opportunities to earn money. Is it because of the government or the states handing out welfare? Could it be the cause, but those are just temporary? Or is it something else? What are your thoughts? But these are my opinions and observations; I believe that people are homeless or stay homeless because they have some mental illness. I'm not saying that the majority of homeless people want to remain homeless, but some who want to be homeless, I believe, have mental issues.

This is where mindfulness comes in. If we are mindful of our situations, we won't be in a place we don't want to be. That is why I am emphasizing the importance of our minds. Mental health is just as important as our physical health. If you think you are having anxiety attacks, stress, destructive behavior, hopelessness, or suicidal behavior, please reach out. I have included some helpful references that you may use in this book.

I agree or disagree with my opinion about homelessness; if a person is thinking straight, then that person does not have to worry about being homeless.

Homelessness is a complex issue that extends far beyond the surface-level explanation of lack of jobs or government assistance. While it may seem that the solution to homelessness is simply providing a job or a home, the root causes are much deeper and more multifaceted. It is important to understand that homelessness is not a one-size-fits-all issue. People experiencing homelessness come from various walks of life, and their reasons for being homeless are often unique to their individual circumstances.

Yes, there are jobs available. There are countless job opportunities across the United States in various industries. However, the reality is that not everyone has the same access to these opportunities. Factors such as education, skills, experience, and even discrimination can create significant barriers to employment. For someone experiencing mental health challenges, addiction, or trauma, even if jobs are available, the ability to hold down a job or even show up for an interview can be daunting. It is not just a matter of showing up for work; it is about the ability to function in a way that society expects, and for many homeless individuals, that ability has been deeply affected by circumstances beyond their control.

In addition to mental health challenges, addiction is another significant factor that often contributes to homelessness. Substance abuse can both result from and contribute to homelessness, creating a vicious cycle. Many individuals struggling with addiction have lost jobs, family, and friends due to their substance use, and finding a way out becomes an insurmountable obstacle. Recovery takes time, and for some, the access to treatment programs, rehabilitation, or supportive communities is simply not available or is out of reach. Without these essential resources, many people end up stuck in a cycle of homelessness and addiction, unable to break free.

Another often overlooked factor in the homelessness crisis is trauma. Many individuals who find themselves on the streets have experienced significant trauma in their lives, whether it be abuse, neglect, or violence. Traumatic experiences can have long-lasting effects on an individual's mental and emotional well-being, often leading to an inability to trust others, difficulty in forming stable relationships, and challenges in maintaining employment or housing. These individuals may find themselves struggling with feelings of worthlessness, anxiety, depression, and even post-traumatic stress disorder (PTSD), which can make the transition from homelessness to stability much more difficult.

While mental illness plays a significant role in homelessness, it is not the sole factor. There are many external factors that contribute to the situation, such as the lack of affordable housing, rising rent prices, and the growing income inequality. As the cost of living continues to rise, many individuals and families find themselves on the brink of homelessness. A single medical emergency, job loss, or unexpected financial hardship can push someone into a situation where they are unable to make rent or afford basic necessities, ultimately leading to eviction and homelessness.

The question remains: why are people homeless? Why do so many individuals find themselves without a place to call home in one of the wealthiest nations on Earth? The answer is not simple, and it requires a deeper examination of society's values, the availability of mental health care, addiction services, and affordable housing, and the systemic issues that contribute to inequality.

Mindfulness plays a significant role in both preventing homelessness and helping individuals who are currently experiencing homelessness.

Mindfulness, in its simplest form, is the ability to be present in the moment and to observe your thoughts and feelings without judgment. It is about taking a step back, assessing your current situation, and making conscious choices about how to move forward. For those struggling with homelessness, mindfulness can help them gain a sense of control over their thoughts and emotions, reduce stress, and build resilience in the face of adversity. It can also assist in recognizing the need for help and accessing the resources available to them.

However, mindfulness alone is not enough. While it can be a valuable tool for coping and mental well-being, addressing the root causes of homelessness requires systemic changes. The government and society as a whole must invest more in mental health services, addiction recovery programs, and affordable housing. These services are essential in helping individuals transition from homelessness to stability, providing not only the physical resources of housing but also the mental and emotional support necessary to rebuild a life.

Homelessness is not just an issue that affects those on the streets; it is a problem that affects all of society. The lack of stable housing, access to healthcare, and job opportunities contributes to a cycle of poverty and marginalization that is difficult to break. As a society, we must look beyond stereotypes and assumptions about homeless individuals and take a closer look at the factors that contribute to their situation. Instead of blaming individuals for their homelessness, we should focus on creating an environment where everyone has the opportunity to thrive.

One of the critical elements in solving homelessness is education. Educating people about the causes of homelessness and the ways in which we can help is an essential step in creating lasting change. It is also crucial to combat the stigma surrounding homelessness. The assumption that all homeless people are lazy or unwilling to work is not only inaccurate but harmful. The vast majority of homeless individuals want to improve their circumstances, but they face immense challenges that can make it incredibly difficult to do so. By providing education, resources, and support, we can help individuals break the cycle of homelessness and empower them to regain control of their lives.

The media also plays a role in shaping the narrative surrounding homelessness. Often, the media perpetuates the stereotype of the "homeless person" as someone who is lazy or unmotivated, failing to address the complex reality of their situation. It is important for the media to highlight the stories of individuals who are working hard to overcome their circumstances, seeking help for mental health or addiction issues, and striving to build a better future for themselves. By shifting the narrative from one of blame to one of empathy and understanding, we can create a more compassionate society that works toward practical solutions.

While the government and society must do more to address homelessness, there is also a role for individuals to play in helping those who are struggling. Volunteering at shelters, donating to organizations that provide services to homeless individuals, or simply offering a kind word or a helping hand can make a significant difference in someone's life. Sometimes, all someone needs is to know that they are seen and valued, even in the midst of their struggles.

At the end of the day, homelessness is a complex issue that requires a multifaceted solution. It is not enough to simply provide jobs or temporary welfare; we must address the underlying causes of homelessness, such as mental health issues, addiction, trauma, and systemic inequality. By working together as a society, we can create a world where no one has to experience homelessness, and where everyone has the opportunity to live a safe, stable, and fulfilling life.

OPINION:

As we all know, we all have different opinions, yet when we open our views to others, no matter how positive they are to others, they come out negative. I notice this a lot whenever I speak to others, and it makes me wonder; it is not that my point of view is negative; it's just that it's different from theirs. And I ask myself, why is that? Through thoughts and observation, I concluded that our upbringing, life experiences, and education play a part in it.

Our point of view, created by our past experiences in life, molds this opinion. So, how can we persuade a person to agree with our opinion? Some of you might say, "Through the power of persuasion." Yes, that is one way. Also, you might try listening to that person and developing an idea that will benefit each other. Each opinion can be positive or negative, depending on the subject matter; remember that different opinions open up more ideas, which is how they create new things.

Why did I bring up this topic of opinion? Personally, whenever I brought up my opinion to others, people responded to me as if it was a negative thing, and that upset me; I felt lost and discouraged, but as I matured and began to understand that that's all it was a different opinion and should not take it as a bad thing and should not hurt our feelings, some of us will get mad or be angry to that person just because of a different opinion, we must accept to agree and disagree no matter what the topic is, we shouldn't close our thoughts to just our own, there are so many ideas out there that can improve the one that we have, be open-minded, because that is how we grow as a person and as a group.

As human beings, we are naturally inclined to view the world through the lens of our own experiences. These experiences are unique to each individual, shaped by factors like culture, family, education, personal challenges, and even our personalities. As a result, it should come as no surprise that our opinions vary greatly from one person to another. Yet, this diversity of thought is what makes conversations, debates, and discussions so rich and meaningful. It's through differing opinions that we can learn, adapt, and grow.

However, the challenge lies in how we respond to those differing opinions. As I've observed in various interactions, there is often a tendency to view someone's opinion as a direct challenge to our own beliefs. This reaction can sometimes lead to misunderstandings, conflict, or even feelings of frustration. This is especially true when a well-meaning conversation turns sour simply because of a difference in perspective. Why does this happen? The reason lies in the nature of human psychology and the way our minds are wired to defend our beliefs.

When we express an opinion, we are essentially sharing a piece of our identity. Our opinions are deeply intertwined with our values, our experiences, and our worldview. As a result, when someone disagrees with us, it can feel as though they are questioning not just our opinion but us as a person. It's no wonder that a simple difference of opinion can sometimes escalate into a heated exchange. However, this reaction is more about emotional defense than rational discourse. The challenge is learning how to navigate those differences in a way that fosters understanding rather than division.

One of the most important lessons I've learned over the years is that a difference of opinion does not equate to a personal attack. Just because someone disagrees with me doesn't mean they are invalidating my beliefs or values. They are simply offering a different perspective based on their own set of experiences and reasoning. By understanding this, I've been able to approach conversations with more patience and open-mindedness.

So how do we persuade someone to agree with our point of view? Is persuasion the right approach? While persuasion is one way to influence others, it's important to remember that changing someone's mind is not always the goal. Sometimes, the purpose of sharing our opinions is simply to communicate our perspective and engage in a thoughtful exchange of ideas. This doesn't mean we need to "win" the conversation or convince the other person to adopt our views. Instead, the aim should be to foster mutual respect, understanding, and empathy.

Active listening plays a crucial role in this process. When we listen carefully to someone's point of view, we not only gain insight into their thought process but also create an environment of respect and collaboration. Often, the key to reaching a common ground lies not in trying to "prove" our opinion but in genuinely understanding the other person's perspective. By asking questions, seeking clarification, and expressing empathy, we can create a space where both parties feel heard and valued, even if they continue to disagree.

It's also important to remember that disagreement doesn't have to lead to conflict. The idea of agreeing to disagree is essential to maintaining healthy relationships and promoting intellectual growth. When we are able to acknowledge that not every conversation will result in consensus, we free ourselves from the need to be right all the time. In fact, it's often through the process of exploring opposing viewpoints that we refine our own beliefs and gain new insights. A willingness to embrace differing opinions can lead to greater creativity, innovation, and problem-solving.

Another aspect to consider is the role of emotional intelligence in navigating differing opinions. Emotions are a natural part of human interaction, but they can sometimes cloud our judgment and make it difficult to engage constructively. By cultivating emotional intelligence, we can better manage our reactions and stay focused on the goal of productive dialogue. Emotional intelligence involves self-awareness, empathy, and the ability to regulate one's emotions in a way that promotes positive communication. When we are able to remain calm and composed, even in the face of disagreement, we create an environment where both parties feel safe to express their opinions without fear of judgment or hostility.

I've come to realize that the ability to agree to disagree is a sign of maturity and wisdom. It requires humility to acknowledge that our perspective is not the only valid one. When we accept that others may have different experiences, values, and viewpoints, we expand our own understanding of the world. This doesn't mean we abandon our own beliefs, but rather that we develop a deeper appreciation for the diversity of thought that exists around us. It is through this appreciation that we grow as individuals and as a society.

In many ways, our opinions are shaped by the times and environments in which we live. For instance, the opinions we hold today may have been influenced by the information available to us, the culture we were raised in, and the events that have shaped our lives. As society evolves and new ideas emerge, our opinions may change over time as well. This is a natural part of the human experience. The key is to remain open to growth and change, to recognize that our beliefs are not fixed but rather fluid and subject to revision as we learn and evolve.

As I reflect on my own experiences, I realize that my perspective on the importance of differing opinions has grown significantly. When I was younger, I was more inclined to dismiss ideas that didn't align with my own. I didn't fully understand the value of hearing from others who thought differently than I did. Over time, however, I've come to appreciate that differing opinions are not threats, but opportunities for learning and growth. I no longer see a disagreement as something to be feared, but as a chance to expand my own understanding.

The beauty of opinion lies in its diversity. It's through the exchange of ideas that we are able to create progress, solve problems, and make meaningful changes in the world. Instead of viewing others' opinions as obstacles to our own, we should view them as stepping stones toward greater understanding. By remaining open-minded, empathetic, and patient, we can create a world where differences of opinion are celebrated rather than feared.

Ultimately, the goal is not to force others to adopt our opinions, but to engage in conversations that challenge and refine our thinking. It's about fostering a culture of respect, curiosity, and mutual understanding. When we approach each conversation with the mindset that every opinion has value, we unlock the potential for growth, connection, and innovation. And perhaps, in doing so, we will find that the diversity of thought is not something to be afraid of, but something to embrace.

In our daily lives, we are constantly bombarded with different opinions, viewpoints, and perspectives from people we encounter. Whether it's from our family, friends, colleagues, or even strangers, the opinions of others can significantly shape our understanding of the world. Yet, it is important to recognize that the opinions we hold are just that — opinions. They are not facts, and they are certainly not universally true for everyone. Understanding this distinction is crucial for fostering more harmonious interactions with others.

One of the most powerful aspects of having a variety of opinions is that it opens up opportunities for growth. When we are exposed to ideas that challenge our own, we are presented with a chance to reflect, reconsider, and perhaps even evolve our thinking. This process of growth requires humility. It requires the willingness to admit that we may not have all the answers and that others may have valuable insights to offer. It is through this vulnerability that we can learn and expand our worldview. If we close ourselves off to new ideas simply because they don't align with our current beliefs, we limit our potential for growth.

This brings us to an important point: change. Our opinions, just like ourselves, are not static. They can evolve over time as we gain new experiences and exposure to different perspectives. In fact, one of the most beautiful aspects of being human is our ability to change and adapt. Our beliefs and opinions are constantly being shaped by our interactions with the world around us. For example, the way we view relationships, politics, or social issues may look completely different today than it did five years ago, and that's okay. The key is not to be afraid of change, but to embrace it as a natural part of our development.

Sometimes, change happens gradually. We may not even realize that our opinions are evolving until we reflect on them later. At other times, however, change can come more suddenly. A major life event, such as the loss of a loved one or a personal challenge, may shift our perspective in profound ways. These moments of change often serve as a catalyst for deep introspection, forcing us to reconsider what we thought we knew and reevaluate the beliefs that have guided us. While these moments can be uncomfortable or even painful, they can also be transformative. They provide us with the opportunity to emerge with a renewed sense of clarity and purpose.

At the same time, it is important to recognize that change does not always mean abandoning our original beliefs. Sometimes, change simply involves refining or expanding upon our existing opinions. For instance, we may have initially held a certain view on a particular topic, but through further education, reflection, and dialogue, we may come to see that the issue is more complex than we originally thought. Instead of completely rejecting our former viewpoint, we can integrate new knowledge and experiences to create a more nuanced understanding.

This approach allows us to grow without losing the essence of who we are.

One of the biggest challenges in navigating differing opinions is learning how to communicate effectively. It is easy to become defensive or combative when someone disagrees with us, especially if we feel strongly about a particular issue. However, the goal of any conversation should not be to "win" or to prove the other person wrong. Rather, the goal should be to foster mutual understanding and respect. Effective communication involves active listening, patience, and empathy. It requires us to listen not just to respond, but to truly understand where the other person is coming from. This level of engagement creates a space where both parties feel valued and heard.

When we approach conversations with a mindset of curiosity and openness, we create an environment where differences of opinion are celebrated rather than feared. This is not to say that we should always agree with one another, but rather that we should approach disagreements with a spirit of collaboration rather than confrontation. By doing so, we increase the likelihood of finding common ground and building stronger, more meaningful relationships. Even if we don't agree on every point, we can still learn from each other and walk away with a greater appreciation for the diversity of thought that exists. In many ways, learning to appreciate differing opinions is a form of emotional maturity. It requires us to set aside our ego and recognize that we are not always right. It requires us to be humble enough to admit when we don't have all the answers and to be open to the possibility that someone else may have a better idea. It also requires us to manage our emotions in a way that allows for productive dialogue. It can be difficult to keep our cool when someone challenges our beliefs, but by practicing emotional regulation, we can remain calm and composed in the face of disagreement.

One of the most powerful tools for cultivating emotional maturity is self-awareness. When we become aware of our emotional triggers and the underlying beliefs that shape our opinions, we gain greater control over how we respond to others. Self-awareness allows us to step back from our emotions and engage in more thoughtful, reflective conversations. It also helps us recognize when our opinions are being influenced by external factors, such as societal pressures or past experiences, rather than objective reasoning. By examining our own biases and assumptions, we can approach discussions with greater clarity and openness.

It's also important to recognize that our opinions are not always a reflection of who we are as individuals. We are not defined solely by what we believe or how we think. Our identities are shaped by a wide range of factors, including our values, our passions, and our actions. While our opinions may evolve over time, they do not determine our worth as people. It's essential to separate our sense of self from our beliefs in order to engage with others in a way that is respectful and constructive.

The beauty of differing opinions is that they challenge us to think critically. When we encounter an opinion that contradicts our own, it forces us to examine our beliefs and consider why we hold them. This process of self-reflection encourages us to become more thoughtful and deliberate in our thinking. It also helps us identify areas where we may need to grow or adjust our perspective. By embracing differing opinions, we open ourselves up to a world of new ideas and possibilities.

One of the greatest benefits of engaging with differing opinions is that it helps us become more empathetic. When we take the time to listen to others and understand their point of view, we develop a deeper sense of compassion for their experiences. We come to realize that everyone's perspective is shaped by their unique circumstances, and that no one's opinion is entirely right or wrong. This understanding fosters a sense of unity and connection, even in the face of disagreement.

Differing opinions are not something to fear or avoid, but something to embrace. They offer us the opportunity to learn, grow, and expand our understanding of the world. By approaching conversations with humility, openness, and empathy, we can create an environment where all perspectives are valued and respected. In doing so, we can foster greater understanding, build stronger relationships, and contribute to a more compassionate and inclusive society. Whether we agree or disagree, the exchange of ideas is what drives progress and innovation. It is through this exchange that we become better versions of ourselves and move closer to a world where diversity of thought is celebrated.

Quote:"An Ounce of prevention is better than a Pound of Cure."

www.ingramcontent.com/pod-product-compliance
Lightning Source LLC
Chambersburg PA
CBHW070027100426
42740CB00013B/2622